The Source

Ursula James

The Source

A Manual
of Everyday Magic

preface
publishing

Published by Preface Publishing 2011

10 9 8 7 6 5 4 3

First published in Great Britain in 2011 by Preface Publishing
20 Vauxhall Bridge Road
London SW1V 2SA

An imprint of The Random House Group Limited

www.rbooks.co.uk

Addresses for companies within The Random House Group Limited can be found at www.randomhouse.co.uk

The Random House Group Limited Reg. No. 954009

A CIP catalogue record for this book is available from the British Library

ISBN 978 1 84809 296 9

Mixed Sources
Product group from well-managed
forests and other controlled sources
www.fsc.org Cert no. TT-COC-2139
© 1996 Forest Stewardship Council

The Random House Group Limited supports The Forest Stewardship Council (FSC), the leading international forest certification organisation. All our titles that are printed on Greenpeace approved FSC certified paper carry the FSC logo. Our paper procurement policy can be found at www.rbooks.co.uk/environment

Printed and bound in Great Britain by Clays Ltd, St Ives PLC

MOTHER SHIPTON'S MOTH

*T*he Mother Shipton moth is not nocturnal, it is often mistaken for a butterfly unless you look closely. Not unlike the witches who move amongst us. It is easy to assume we are all butterflies. Sometimes it pays to look more closely.

To the one constant in the storm of my life.
This one is for you, Phil.
My love to you now, and for ever.

ACKNOWLEDGEMENTS

I am now fortunate enough to have in my life some wonderful people who keep me (relatively, and I do use that word on purpose) sane.

My thanks to the inner circle of women who surround me with love: specifically Lorraine Flaherty, Elizabeth Limb, Mirela Hodzig, Sue Sayer and those who prefer me not to name them here, but you know who you are.

To all of you, I hope you know that I am there for you when you need me.

And to those whose knowledge and care from which I have been fortunate enough to benefit: Nicola Ibison, Rina Gill, Ashleigh Fleming, Emanuela Tebaldi, Jo Wander, and not forgetting Rob Shore who has had to learn a whole new language to become part of the magic.

Bless you all for your generosity.

For Trevor Dolby at Random House, who added his own form of magic to this volume, and saw further than those around him to push for publication.

My thanks, also, to Jonathan Conway of Mulcahy Conway Associates for having enough of Mother Moon in him to understand the magic.

Finally, to all the carers in this world – paid and unpaid – who care for the sick, the dying, the vulnerable, the young and the old. This book is for you, most of all.

Ursula James, Pays-de-la-Loire, June 2010

AUTHOR'S NOTE

$\mathcal{U}$rsula Sontheil, known as Mother Shipton, was a famed healer and prophetess in the county of Yorkshire in the north of England. She lived in the reign of King Henry VIII, and some say she was burned as a witch by Cardinal Wolsey for prophesying that he would never get to see York. As it turned out he didn't, for on his way there he was called back to London accused of treason, and died en route. Mother Shipton's spirit was trapped in a cave in Knaresborough, North Yorkshire. The cave has an unusual characteristic: anything taken there is turned to stone by the action of the lime-suffused waters from a nearby well. Mother Shipton used this water to create an image of herself in the cave, and then split the cave open to call the needy. Sick at heart or in body, people came to her in the cave to offer her objects in return for her healing powers. Mother Shipton is said to have accurately prophesied many things, from the two world wars to the internet, and stories of her magical abilities continued long after her death. At times of strife in England, her prophecies were avidly consulted. Now she and her magic are almost forgotten, but for one woman she is very much alive and still weaving magical spells.

Ursula James was also born in Yorkshire. She is a visiting teaching fellow at Oxford University Medical School and an honorary lecturer at Barts and the London School of Medicine and Dentistry, where she teaches clinical hypnosis to future doctors. She is working on a PhD in biomedical sciences and conducts medical research. Her work *The Clinical Hypnosis Textbook* is the first textbook on hypnosis for medical students. She is a practical sort of woman, not the type you would think communicates with witches, especially dead ones. However, since her childhood, Mother Shipton has talked to her and guided her steps. As a child, Ursula didn't think this was at all unusual, but she soon learned to keep silent about Mother, and as she grew, shut her out of her life. Until, that is, the time came when she craved magic once again.

The Source: A Manual of Everyday Magic tells of how Ursula James called on Ursula Sontheil through the centuries to make her life magical. It is a tale of the arrogance of the modern age, and how Ursula James finally learned how to trust in true magic – anima magic – and through it to get what she wanted out of life and more. Mother Shipton's prophecies, as channeled to the reader by Ursula James, provide spells for, as Kaballah says, *tikkun olam* – the healing of the world. The prophecies speak of relationships, love, the power of forgiveness, how to heal your own world and then make the connections with others to help them heal theirs.

    The Source comes out of time and is of this time. It is only now, with the world of commerce in free fall, that we are ready to listen and respond to Sister Moon and to heal Mother Earth. Part fable, part spell book, *The Source* has true magic laced through it, and the magic can heal those who read it well. Each chapter includes rituals, rites or spells, guiding readers to the source of their power. Comparisons with *The Celestine Prophecy* or *The Secret* are inevitable. This book, however, is different. Both Mother Shipton and Ursula James are real. Read it and learn how to make magic real. Read it and change the world.

CONTENTS

PROLOGUE

The First Lesson

✠

Have you ever wanted magic to be real? I mean truly real? For there to be a force of nature which could transform your life into something amazing? It exists. It lies dormant in these pages until you read the words of power and let the magic loose into your life. Make no mistake, the words will change your life. You will become part of the magic – one with the Source – and you will meet others who are magical creatures too.

It took me a lifetime to accept the magic into my life, and now it is part of me I have no choice but to pass that knowledge on. That is part of the deal with true magic. It must be shared.

My name is Ursula James and I hypnotise people for a living. I am a successful therapist – good at what I do and well respected for it. I breathe the same air that you do. I live on your world, but not in it. I am successful, not just in my career, but in my life too. I had a good teacher, although for my first thirteen years I did not pay attention to her, and it took another twenty before I was prepared to listen again. By then I had undergone my own learning and was ready to hear and understand her words.

Mother Shipton was my teacher, my healer, my guide. She would come to me in sleep and in dreams, but it was only when I learned how to hypnotise myself that she came through to me fully formed and separate from my own inner voice. I can tell you now that was a very strange day. I was in hypnosis, preparing myself for the day, when she started to talk. It wasn't that I hadn't heard her before, because she had always been with me. It was more that I had tuned her out of my thoughts. When we are children we are open to the voices. We are open to the impressions of the air around us. We use our senses fully until we are taught not to. As we grow up, we stop listening and close our senses to the world around us.

You may think me odd, but this book is not about your thoughts. I care for your feelings – your needs. Just as Mother Shipton did – just as she still does. It is through me that her story will be told, and you will start to hear her voice again – if you are open to the magic around you. The magic of the earth. True, deep magic. That which lies in the belly of everyone. This is why I am writing to you now, to tell you how you can reclaim your magic. I can see into your hearts just as Mother did. You want your power. You want magic to be real – it is just that for now part of you is afraid. Afraid to connect. Afraid to plug into your Source. Maybe even afraid of yourself. There is no need to fear any more. You are not alone. I have connected to the Source and I know that there is nothing to fear when you do. You can and will be free. Through my voice, Mother will teach you. Mother is with you. I am with you.

The simple steps and paths which you will discover in these pages will lead you to the Source of your power and help you to harness it. Believe me now as I stand within the Source, you will know when you have connected to the Source, and the power will never leave you when you have brought it back within you. **For there is your first lesson – the Source is within you, and without you it dies.** First you must recognise its existence, find it within you, then nurture and strengthen it. Only then can you start to use it, and when you do you will be free. Free from the chains of commerce that you believe bind you. Free to give and receive love, to heal the world around you, and to make things happen around you. That is true magic, to take the clay of your life and model it in your hands. Above all you will have the strength in mind and body to share the Source with others.

It is not an easy journey, but I can tell you that it is worthwhile. Before I listened to Mother and connected with the Source I lived a different life – a life as far from full as the difference between a grainy black-and-white photograph and actually being there. This is where my story begins.

I thought I knew it all – really I did. I was working hard, I was doing well professionally. So what if I didn't have a partner and my friends didn't invite me out any more because I was too busy? That's what life can be like in London. That's what happens when you get successful. So, I would spend my way out of registering the feelings which were growing inside me. Feelings of darkness and loneliness. Feelings of pain. I would take myself out of London and sit on a beautiful beach in Thailand or India and try to be real. It was an effort. All of it. I was no longer in my own head or my body, and had lost all respect for myself and sight of where I was going. It didn't matter where I went, I went with me, and I started to detest it. The inner voice of self-loathing grew louder and louder, until I felt as if the whole world must be able to hear the battle going on inside. I walked the streets of London. I sat outside in the freezing cold with my latte and newspaper. So self-possessed. So chic. So dead. It took a number to change it.

The number for me was forty. The age I was about to become. I didn't want to be forty – anything but. To me, reaching that number without children or a partner in my life, without love and people to share with felt like a failure. I had made it professionally. I was doing well, I was good at what I did, people *seemed* to respond to me – but it all felt empty. I wasn't rich enough to give up work nor was I at the top of my profession. Close – but no cigar. Any victory I could claim felt hollow and brittle. I knew that if I was brave enough to look forward in time

I would see my life progressing on the same course for the next forty years until I was old, worn out and bitter. At best I could cultivate my oddness, my eccentricity and make a virtue out of it as if I had chosen it, really I had. The worst of it was that I could feel the bitterness already – I could taste it in my mouth like bile. I felt unhealthy and bone-weary.

So, I took myself up to a Buddhist retreat in Scotland. I usually did a spa every year. It would be good to try something different for a change. What I hadn't bargained for was the cold – God, was it cold – and *so* gloomy. Everything seemed grey and squashed beneath the sky. Surely this was a mistake. It was supposed to be summer, for goodness' sake. I remember looking around at the people who were there with a mild disdain. What was I doing? This place wasn't for me – no soft towels, no bubbly spa, no elegant food, no alcohol! And the people, well there was just no one here to connect with. No one from my world who could be useful to me when I got back to London. No point in networking at all. Ah well, I was here now. At least I could catch up on some sleep. Thing was, I wasn't going to be given the chance.

This was spiritualist boot camp. I was woken on the first day to join the walking meditation group. At least I had asked for a silent retreat so I wouldn't have to communicate with any of these dreadful people. I dragged myself out of bed, and joined the end of the snake of people making its way into the forest. Pissed off and shivering, I followed instructions as a female voice whispered in my ear. 'Step only in the footsteps of the one who walks before you.' Her own feet were sandalled and dirty. When I looked up to see her face she was gone. I started to walk – well stomp, to be accurate. I walked like a grumpy child, head down and arms wrapped tightly around myself. It took a while, but gradually the feelings of irritation started to wear off, and I began to take in my surroundings – making a game of placing my tiny feet into the tread made by the boots of the man before me. It was like when you're little, and you avoid the cracks in the pavement because you know that if you don't step on them you can make something wonderful happen. Little rituals that calm you. When did I stop doing that?

In my musing I walked straight into the back of the man before me. We had stopped walking and I hadn't noticed. He turned around and reached out his hand to steady me. It felt rough and dry, like the bark of a tree. He smiled and turned his back on me again. It was the weirdest feeling – I wanted to cry. I wanted to take his hand in mine and carefully drop the tears into his palm. Oh yes – I was sure of it then. I was definitely starting to lose the plot, and the sooner I got away from this place the better. I needed to go back to London now. That was it. I would go home and everything would be all right again. The snake of people set off again, and the path got steeper. I was getting tired – my legs were starting to ache and I still wanted to cry. This was too ridiculous. When we got back I would find someone in charge and they could arrange for a taxi to collect me. I couldn't stay here any longer. I walked for hours and hours – until the forest started to give way to rocks and heather. The air hurt my lungs. I couldn't think properly. I tried to list all the things that I was going to do when I got back home to London, but the thoughts wouldn't come. I was walking in a dream now. The words faded and my mind became blank and empty – my body went on autopilot. Nothing else mattered, except to keep walking. I concentrated on the footprints and time passed without meaning. I wanted to cry so badly now it was beginning to hurt, and I just couldn't think why. I did try. I tried to remember where the pain came from, and why it was so urgent for me to leave this place, but I couldn't remember that either. It felt like hours had passed by now, but I had no way of telling.

Finally I looked up – I had left the forest and I was alone on a hill. I had walked halfway up the mountain. I could see the tilted roof of the retreat down below me and feel the strength of the mountain rising behind. I sat down on a rock – and cried.

I cried for myself, and for the life I felt I had missed. I cried because somehow I had lost the path. I cried because I was alone and I hadn't noticed when it had happened. I cried ugly, unselfconscious tears, the kind that mark your eyes the next day and leave you looking like a frog. I cried until I was exhausted. I slept right there, curled up in the heather like an animal. I could feel the wind on my cheeks, and the clumps of heather pushing at my body. I slept until the rain woke me. Big fat drops of rain hit my face, and I began to laugh. Sitting up I could see the sun dropping away on the horizon, red splattered clouds around it. The sky was really beautiful – so beautiful. This was a beauty I couldn't capture with a camera and take home with me. This was nature's show – vast and unique, and I was the only spectator. It sounds like such a cliché, but it was true for me that day. For the first time in my life I felt connected to the earth, every part of it. I felt different, but I still didn't know quite how different I was.

Walking back down the hill through the path in the forest I knew that something had changed inside me, and I thought this change was something I could carry back into my old life, as if the visit to the mountain had been no more than an interlude. If I had known *how* different I would become as a result I might have thought twice about coming back down off the mountain. Hindsight is a wonderful gift, and as I read my words I notice that all I talk about is my thoughts, but this had nothing to do with my thoughts. My thoughts were irrelevant here. My feelings drove me up the mountain, and my feelings drive me now. This was an old lesson – one Mother had tried to teach me as a child, but education was all that mattered to me then. Education, education, education. I bought into the lie, and forgot to feel. No matter. The lesson got learned later, that's all.

I came down the mountain, cold and hungry and ready to feel. I washed quickly and made my way to the eating room. Food was shared out in silence, and I looked out for my companion from the hill. He wasn't there. For some reason I felt disappointed. I wanted to communicate with him. To smile at him. Instead I looked at those around me on that long, worn table for the first time. A woman to my right smiled at me cautiously. I smiled back and touched the back of her forearm with my hand, pointing over to the bread with the other. She gestured to the other side of the table, and the bread found its way into my hand. I smiled at her, and dipped the rough bread into my bowl of soup. The food that day tasted like nothing I can describe to you. I could taste the love with which it had been made, the care with which it had been served, the friendship with which it had been apportioned out to those around the table.

When the meal was over, I picked up a tray from the sideboard and started to collect the empty bowls and spoons. The woman sat opposite me did the same. Someone picked up a cloth and wiped the table. Another started to sweep the floor, brushing the remaining crumbs out of the door. I started to wash the dishes, then halfway through was gently moved aside as someone else took over. Every task got completed. No instructions. No words. There was a gentle rhythm to it all, like birdsong – seemingly without structure but complete and beautiful. I returned to the dining room, then walked through it to the heart of the building – a large round room with an open fireplace. People were already gathering around the fire. Some were reading, others watched the fire with eyes half closed. I found myself an armchair away from the fire so I could sit in the shadows. I didn't want light or conversation, nor did I want to go straight to my solitary room. I wanted to be around other people, to feel them. My eyes started to close, and yet again I could not hold on to a single thread of thought. It was the strangest sensation, like floating in a salt lake with no sense of your body, but with this feeling I was losing my sense of self. For some reason that didn't bother me, although a small past voice dressed in a suit told me that it should matter. I blew on the figure and she disappeared as if made from mist. My old self. Suited and serious. Brittle and fragile – and, if I wanted to be brutally honest, a bit of a pain in the arse. She *had* to be right. Had to be in charge. She always knew best. I decided there and then that she really needed a rest. Not a break, but she needed to be put to rest. She deserved it. That much was certain, so I took her back up the mountain and let her sleep – there on the mountain where she could be safe and free. I surrounded her with summer sun and flowers, and let her hair grow long and beautiful. I dressed her in a long velvet dress, like a princess from a fairy tale, and I put her into an enchanted sleep. All this while dozing in the shadows, unseen and unheard. I stayed until the fire burned out, and I knew she was safe on the mountain.

That night I slept so heavily. I slept on a narrow bed with hard scratchy sheets. I slept better that night than I had in the finest hotels in the world, and when I woke I felt alive and awake, and ready to do things. Yes, I know – *do things* is a little vague, but that is all I could think that day. I didn't have a plan, just lots of energy. So I cooked and cleaned. I swept leaves. I dusted and polished the bookshelves in the library. I felt as if I had been wired to the national grid. This continued for the three days of my stay. Each night I slept soundly and without dreams. Each day I worked on whatever needed doing. By the end of the three days I knew all of my companions by name – well, names I had given them, anyway. Blue hat. Aztec scarf. Bell earrings. I wondered what they called me. I never did find out. By the third night, new faces arrived around the table, and it was time for me to leave. The next day I cleared out my room, bundled the sheets up and took them down to the laundry. With his back to me I recognised him. It was my pathmaker. I handed him the sheets and he opened his arms to me and held me without words. I looked up into his face. He had beautiful blue eyes, crinkled all round with laughter. Clear blue eyes like the sky over my old self on the mountain. He turned back to his work and I left for London.

The journey back by train was uneventful. I turned on my mobile and let the world come back in. Lots of voice messages. Lots of emails. I must be important. I turned it off again and spent the rest of the journey staring through the window. Back home, nothing had changed, and that surprised me. I had, why hadn't my surroundings? Okay, I know. It's one thing to have a spiritual experience when you are away from home, but then you have to deal with reality. Your reality – as created by you. That was the thing, really – I was still living in her house, wearing her clothes, and living her life. Not only did it feel wrong, but I wasn't even sure if I could *pretend* to be her any more. It was as if by leaving her on the mountain I had also left her ways of doing things behind me – and I didn't have a clue what I was supposed to do now. I only knew what I *didn't* want. I did not yet know what I did want. So I did the only thing I could do, and that was to open her diary and see what she was supposed to be doing this week. It was a busy one. It would be. She had hypnotherapy clients booked for the entire week. That meant I wouldn't see daylight until Saturday. So I got on with it. I dressed in her clothes, spoke her words, comforted her clients. By the time Saturday came my head was stuffed full of other people's sadness and grief, anger and pain. I needed to decant it, and quickly. I decided to do some self-hypnosis to tidy up my thoughts. Saturday morning came, and I lay on the bed in the sunlight from the skylight above me and closed my eyes in preparation. That's when Mother came to me. Fully formed, loud and clear, and in glorious Technicolor. *Morning,* she said convivially. *Ready to listen now?*

CHAPTER 2

I would love to be able to tell you that my experience on the mountain had prepared me for this, and I had reached some Zen type of acceptance – that I took it all in my stride. I didn't. I screamed and opened my eyes. *Morning,* she repeated. *I'm still here.* With my eyes open, I couldn't see her, exactly, but I could *feel* her, sitting on the edge of the bed. Believe me, I know how it sounds, and my first reaction was to get myself off to the hospital immediately to get my brain scanned because I was obviously having some sort of psychotic episode – or maybe I had a brain tumour, or was I having a stroke, perhaps? I held my breath. All was quiet. Maybe I had eaten some dodgy mushroom in Scotland and I was having some kind of delayed hallucination. Yes – that was probably it. Drugs. I lay back on the bed and closed my eyes, taking a deep breath of relief. My relief was short lived. *Look, we don't have time for this. You are not drugged, you are not ill, and you are not insane. We have work to do. Can we get on with it now?*

With my eyes closed I scanned the room. I could see her then. She was sitting on the bed, watching me. The first thing I noticed was that she was much smaller than I remembered, but I suppose that would be the case as when I had seen her last it was me who had been so much smaller. I stopped seeing and hearing her when I ran out of childhood. To be more accurate I stopped up the ways in so she couldn't get to me any more. I plugged up my dreams and no longer visited the landscape of my mind where we used to go for walks together. I tuned out her signal and let in the voice of man and logic instead. I didn't miss her – I was much too busy. Too busy learning and then too busy earning. Too busy being important, but I should have known better. She hadn't gone away at all, she was just waiting. Of course she was. She had waited five hundred years in a cave for me, she wasn't about to go away just because I wanted her to.

What do you want from me? I said, or rather the voice in my head said. She laughed. It was a beautiful, rich and surprisingly young sound. *You have got that arse-about-face – haven't you, child? It is not what I want from you, but your needs what made me fetch up here.* She paused and stroked the sheet gently. *Nice linen. Good quality.* She broke away from her reverie. *Right, child. You want magic in your life, and I am willing to teach you. The price you pay for my wisdom is that you* must *share it. Keep it to yourself and your powers will wither and fail. Share it with your sisters and the men with enough of Luna in them to be able to harken and you will become a magical creature – exciting and animal, proud and true. I can aid you make this your time, and you will do it by writing. You will take yourself deep into the land of hypnosis, and I will share my magic with you there. You will allow me to use your hand to write and your mind to interpret my words so your sisters and true brothers will understand me. You will be the instrument and I will write through you.* I found myself shivering as she spoke. All the while, her voice grew stronger as my desire for her gift grew too in strength. Could it be possible? Could Mother Shipton call across time and teach, because this is who it was, sitting bolt upright on my bed – a long-dead witch, one of the most famous in England – and anyway, why would I want to listen? *Your link to the male has grown strong. Child. Your logical, analytical, 'I will believe it when I see it' mind may be a barrier for you. We shall see. Are you ready to believe in magic – to make things happen, to be an enchantress? To use your language –* call me! She laughed, and the laughter faded into the sound of branches beating against the skylight. I opened my eyes and looked up. She was gone. I couldn't see her, or hear her, or feel her any more.

I lay on the bed for an hour or more, thinking. The more I thought about it, the less comfortable I was with the whole idea. The entire situation was fraught with trouble. Trouble – the word didn't even come close to describing what was happening to me. Point number one: I am talking to myself. Point number two: I think there is someone else in my head. Point number three: I am contemplating carrying out the suggestions being made by this other voice. Diagnosis – mental illness. No question. I obviously need therapy and drugs. Lots of them probably. Great. Just what I needed, to lose the plot when things are going so well for me. I stared out through the skylight at the dusky clouds beginning to form. But things weren't all going well, were they? I was lonely and unhappy and bored with my life. I was isolated and moody and petty. I was ... Okay, enough self-flagellation, it never suited me. I had always preferred action over analysis. I had arrived at this place where I was supposed to be happy and I wasn't. This was not what I had bought into. I had the car and the house and the oak floorboards and the Smeg fridge and I *still* wasn't happy. What the hell was wrong with me? Had I missed a bit somewhere, the part where you have an inner life, the bit where you become happy – and, dare I even say it – content? One thing was for certain, I couldn't go back to the old version of me. I had lost the capacity to be that person. She was resting peacefully on a mountainside, safe and protected. I didn't feel mad, not crazy mad anyway. Mother had come to me as a child and taught me, why not now? My mind was made up. At least it would be interesting ...

I lay there in the gathering dusk, waiting for her to come back. She didn't. Eventually I fell asleep and dreamed for the first time in years. The dreams were vague but beautiful, impressions of a melancholy tone. I didn't feel sad exactly, but more like the poor kid in the Victorian novels pressing my

nose up against the toyshop window while inside the adored
children with rich parents choose their treats. Was that it? Was
I always going to be on the outside, looking in, or could I walk
into the shop and make myself happy? The dreams continued
through the night, cycling through my sleep. I woke early, with
a banging heart and the feeling that I had forgotten something
really important and that if I didn't remember it there would be
hell to pay. My head hurt, and I felt exhausted, like I had a cold
coming on. Later, washed and dressed, I picked at my muesli.
It had no taste at all. I pushed the bowl away. I'm eating dust
and water, for goodness' sake. How can that make me happy?
I was starting to get irritated by small things. My apparent
choices like eating muesli for breakfast. Was it a choice or was
I conforming? Why was I eating food that did not nourish me,
just because other people told me that was the correct thing to
do? I threw the sorry mess into the waste disposal, and walked
to Ozzies Caff off Marylebone High Street. There I ate the first
'full English' that I had tasted in years. It was bliss. I picked
up a newspaper that someone had left on the seat, and read
about the doom and gloom in England. Don't do this, don't do
that, the world is terrible, the English are being preyed upon
by terrorists, asylum seekers, work-shy lying lowlifes who bleed
our country dry and on, and on, and on. I had a second cup of
tea and started the paper again, scanning for one bit of good
news, one small redeeming feature – one kitten rescued from
a well in Dorset. It wasn't there. I started to feel sorry for the
people who read this paper every day. How could you be happy
when you were letting this into your life? How did they ever
leave the house for fear? It wasn't just this rag – it was all of
them. Preaching the gospel of fear and hate to the masses. Okay
– there were some exceptions – but sadly they proselytised to
their own version of the converted. Smug eco-preachy nimbies.
What was happening to me? I felt as if I was the only person
who could see that the whole of the British press was on a
campaign trail. Not to tell news, but to keep groups apart from

each other. Social cohesion in a daily paper. Pick your group and stick with it. Only read what confirms your long-held beliefs. Do not challenge yourself because it then means that you are going to have to think, to change, to do something about it.

Breakfast paid for, I decided to let my Saturday drift. There had been no personal calls while I had been away. Said it all, really. I could disappear tomorrow and no one would *really* mind too much. Maybe some of my clients would have a momentary blip, but they would soon find someone else to listen to their problems. Mother was spot on about one thing: I wanted magic in my life very badly indeed. I wanted special things to happen around me – I wanted to feel alive, something which was completely lacking right now. Trouble was, I didn't *really* believe in it – magic that is. Magic was for people who wouldn't take responsibility for their own lives, their own happiness – right? Magic was for dreamers and wasters – people who hung plastic fairies from their rear-view mirror and wore Indian print dresses and cardigans. I did not fit into that category, ergo I couldn't possibly believe in it. All that aside, the breakfast had filled me, and I felt happy and satisfied. I walked through Hyde Park then down Exhibition Road, and mooched around in a bookshop there. It was a *proper* shop – not a chain. Inside, it was slightly tatty and overcrowded. It smelt of book. The girl behind the counter was reading, and when she rose to serve a customer she made comments on their choice of book. I loved it in there. Being there made me feel Bohemian and intellectual. What a fraud. I bought a book anyway, something with a beautiful cover about travels in India at the end of the 1800s. I would go home and escape into its pages.

And so it was that my Saturday drifted on. For my lunch I went to Paul's in Marylebone and ate rich sweet cake and drank proper caffeinated coffee with full-fat milk and extra sugar. I could feel my eyes rolling in pleasure and wanted to stamp my feet like a child in excitement at my own naughtiness. I was having a great day. Simple pleasures – guilty pleasures. I knew

I would regret it later when I stepped on the scales, but for once I didn't give a damn. Okay, Scarlett – tomorrow is another day – Sunday as a matter of fact, and you can do it all over again. My weekend went by in an orgy of food and reading. I ate only what I wanted, accompanied my evening meal with champagne, and wore my best underwear and high heels even though there was no one there to see them. I wanted to be the kid inside the shop, not outside. At least for the weekend I could pretend. Sunday evening came, and I laid out my clothes for Monday. Lecturing all day. A whole day of medical students questioning and eager, or bored and resentful. It was my job to feed knowledge into their heads. The thought brought me no joy. My beautiful Vivienne Westwood suit hung empty and limp like a marionette with the stockings and high-heeled patent court shoes laid out neatly close by. Her uniform. The clothes the others responded to when talking to Ursula. To be truthful, I know the clothes had been chosen specifically to have others draw certain impressions. Strong, ballsy, sexy but in an intimidating/controlling sort of way – borderline sado-masochistic. So people saw the image and bought into it. Why should they look any further? People see what they want to see and I had created that Ursula just as effectively as a writer creates a character in a book. Created with broad brushstrokes so the reader can flesh out the gaps in their own image.

I went through the week on automatic. Lectures, clients, meetings. Lectures, clients, meetings. All the while part of me was screaming out, 'Look at me – I'm different! I'm not who you think I am! I don't know who I am but I know who I am *not* any more.' Still they reacted to the suit, and the voice, and the high-heeled shoes, and all through the week I slept badly, dreaming of the inner landscape I used to visit as a child, but not able to go there yet. All week I ate whatever I wanted to eat, and went nowhere near the scales. I was too scared.

Finally Saturday came to visit my home again, and this

time I was ready. Books, food, pyjamas. Door locked. I wasn't going anywhere. Whatever all this stuff was that was happening to me, I needed time to think. Time to make a plan and get on with it. I had my Moleskine notebook and best Lamy pen ready, propped myself up on every cushion I could find and sat cross-legged and pyjama'd on the bed, pen poised over the virgin page. Nothing happened. Absolutely bugger all. I flipped back the page to the front of the notebook and wrote my name carefully on the line where it said 'Name'. I flipped forward and tried again. 'PROBLEMS'. I wrote in capital letters. Then I went to the back of the book and wrote another header. 'SOLUTIONS'. Well, it was a start. I flipped back to the 'PROBLEMS' page and stared at it. Ten minutes. Twenty minutes. Half an hour went by and I was ready – poised to write it all down. Finally I wrote, '*I want magic to be real.*' Hmmm, didn't expect that. Quick flick through to 'SOLUTIONS'. '*Call Mother.*' I wrote. I threw the book to the end of the bed and sprawled out on my back looking once more through the skylight at the clouds above. I drifted. In the end I did the only thing I could think of, and that was to go on the bathroom scales and see how much damage my binge had done. I climbed on, holding my breath (as if it helps), and looked down. I had lost three pounds in weight. I climbed off again, and reset the dial. Nope, there was no mistake. I had eaten whatever I wanted to all week and had not gained an ounce – I had actually lost weight. If Mother was trying to send me a message that magic was real she had got it through in one. There is nothing like losing weight without trying to make a woman sit up and listen. *Okay, Mother. I am calling you right now. I hate myself and my life and I want to believe in magic. Can you hear me?* I stepped off the scales. Nothing. Great. I was losing weight *and* my marbles all at the same time.

Not very patient, are you, child? Mother was sitting on my bed, smiling at me. *It's not like dialling the phone and expecting me to be sitting next to it waiting for your call. I am a busy woman, you know.* Her smile widened. *Yes, I know about phones and the internet and television. I have been able to hear and observe as the world has 'developed'.* She wrinkled her nose at the last word. *Developed but not changed – I think. Child, it is time for you to discover your true self. I will guide and instruct you, but this time bloody well listen. I do not take kindly to being shut out. I allowed it as you were a child then. You are a child no longer and I will treat you as an adult. It is time to make magic.* I sat down beside her. *Did you make me lose all the weight – even though I have been indulging myself all week? No, you did. You momentarily let the idea of magic rest in your mind. You made that happen. Let the male way come back into your thoughts and you will talk the weight back on again.* I opened my mouth with more questions. *No more questions. We do this my way.*

My way meant that she would use my hand whilst I was in hypnosis to automatically put down her words. There would be no filter of my conscious awareness. I would not be allowed to know what she was writing until it had been put down in its entirety by her. I agreed to her terms. What had I got to lose? Okay – my reputation, my clients, my financial security. That's all. I didn't care. I felt so empty and tired, and aware that no one would really miss me if I disappeared tomorrow that it felt worth it. What would you give up for a little magic in your life? For the ability to make things happen – make wonderful things appear in your life and terrible ones fade out? It had to be worth it. If I had lost the plot and gone completely bonkers I had already lost everything anyway, so I created the time and the space for her to use me as the tool for getting her magical story out there into the real world.

From then on it was quite simple. I would take myself into hypnosis and meet Mother in the countryside where we used to walk when I was a child. She would talk to me of nature as we walked, pointing out useful herbs and flowers. Just like we used to. She would test me to see how much I had remembered about the significance of each season and Moon phase. When our walk finally carried us to the house where she had lived as a child with Agatha, her mother, she would make a fire and we would sit together. Then she took my hand and carried it over the page. Her magic was to come out in my hand. Not my handwriting, though. The writing was distinctly hers. Large, scratchy and florid. It was a slow process as it took me a long time to tear my eyes away from the page and allow her to write unseen by me. I wanted to look, but she wouldn't let me. She said that if I did I would start to influence the words – turn them into something different. She kept telling me that the male in me was so strong it could be the ruin of me, and I knew what she meant. The temptation to peek was very strong – but I resisted it. And all the while I continued on my normal course. In my day-to-day life of teaching, seeing clients and having meetings. Business, busyness as usual. The Moleskine was starting to get full, so I bought another. I had asked Mother a couple of times how long it would all take to complete, and when I could look, but she stared at me from her seat by the fireplace until my question faded in my throat. I knew what her response would be: *it will take as long as it takes.* I was starting to get restless and impatient. It had been seven months since my birthday and taking leave of myself on the mountain. I wanted to get on with my new life. Another two months and three Moleskines later, I walked beside Mother to Agatha's house. She went past it and I followed her through the cornfield and to the foothills, where she sat down on a rock, waiting for me to catch up with her.

It is done. She motioned me to sit down beside her. I did, looking out at the gentle valley with its farm and village in the distance. *This is my world. Its boundaries are without limit. In here I can fly anywhere I wish. There is no time here, either. I visit your world as easily as the farmer took me on his cart to York.* I watched the shadow of the clouds moving over the hills in the distance. *I free you from your charge, now. You can now take the books and learn from them. Then you must write it down for others to learn. Share the knowledge – remember that. With any luck you will not hear from me again.* I turned to face her but she was gone,

and I was no longer on the hillside, but back in my bedroom
with the pen still in my hand. It ached. I had almost forgotten
the joy of writing by hand, but now my hand was cramped like
an old woman's. I put the Moleskines together into my bureau
drawer and ran a bath. Not just any old bath – candles, incense,
bubbles, music. I deserved it. The Moleskines could wait.

I left the notebooks there for three weeks until I was ready. I
took a holiday from work, cleared my diary and prepared myself
to learn. When I started to read, I soon realised that there was
a very logical structure to it all. It was practical and methodical,
and would easily translate into a modern piece of writing. In
and among the method was Mother's own story, but I decided
that it wasn't relevant or necessary to share that part of the
writing. It would only confuse and slow down the narrative.
The method would take work, but I knew I could do it. First I
would learn it for myself. I would be the guinea-pig – after all,
who would want to read a book about magic if the author wasn't
themself magical, if they hadn't used it to transform their own
life? This was surely what Mother wanted me to do. She didn't
come again, even when I tried to visit her home – I couldn't
quite make it there. She was stopping up the ways in, just as I
had with her all those years ago when I was a child. Fair enough.
She wouldn't want to be bothered by my questions. I had the
knowledge now – it was up to me to use it.

+

CHAPTER 3

*Y*ou will forgive me if it seems like everything written so far has been a distraction, a diversion. If you wanted magic in your life as much as I did you will allow me to set the scene properly before I write down the contents of Mother's books. I want you to know that I am neither bonkers, nor a fraud. In fact I am a very logical practical person. And that is how my first mistake got made. I could have reached the Source much sooner, but in my rush I thought that I already knew the way there. My own way – of course. Just as you want to get on with making magic. Wait, read. Learn from my mistake. I can admit to it now – although I really don't want to, I have to. Actually, the full confession can wait a little while longer. I just want you to know that magic didn't make me perfect – far from it – the first thing it did was show me my flaws. As it did with me, so it will with you. Some people falter on their way to the Source at this first hurdle. Learn from my mistake. You will make your own on the way, but *it doesn't matter how you get there – your journey will be unique to you*. It is the journey that counts here. Besides, I am sure you are much more interested in whether Mother's magic worked for me. Did it work for me? It did. Oh boy did it work. My life turned around completely. I got *exactly* what I wanted. No catches, no payback, no unpleasant surprises waiting to bite me on the bum. Actually there was one, and that was completely my own fault. I will admit to it – as I said, I have no choice.

So. What did I do with the knowledge Mother had passed

on to me in her writings? Mother had by now closed off all
access to her, and I was alone with the words. There was no
thunder and lightning when I opened them to read, only the
sound of her voice as she relayed the magic to me. Magic lay
spread out before me like a map. Where to go, how to get there,
what to do first. I found myself starting to get excited. If what
Mother had laid down on these pages was true, I could make
myself into a rich, fulfilled woman, with the life I wanted and
the love I craved. This much I hadn't admitted to, even to
Mother. I wanted a man in my life – a true life partner. Deep
down in a secret Mills & Boon corner of my heart I wanted the
full package – thank you very much. It was incredible to me
that I had managed to cling on to that romantic image even
through one failed marriage and a life in the most cynical of
cities – London. What did I do first? I bought myself a brand-
new Moleskine to write in. This would be my story now. I would
put down exactly what I had done and how I had done it. I
would make the first step towards the magic by writing it down.
Giving the words a life of their own so that they could be free
to find other words to make the magic happen. This is what I
wrote:

> I want a mews house in central London
> I want a house in the countryside in France
> I want a marriage to a good man who loves me for who I am
> I want a partner who is interesting as a person
> I want financial freedom
> I want a two-book deal with a major publisher
> I want a series on prime-time TV
> I want a successful training company
> I want my health back
> I want an inner life
> I want to get involved in charity work
> I want to be excited every day
> I want more free time

I want genuine friends
I want to get involved in medical research
I want all of the above in the next two years

I want, I want, I want. I was starting to scare myself. All those things I had written down. Bearing in mind that I was in negative equity in my fiendishly expensive central London apartment, which had legionnaires' disease in the plumbing and a short lease with no possibility of an extension. I had no savings. I had a job that ground me down and left me no time for life. I had no partner, no friends – I had no time for either. I had no contacts in the media world and had never published or gone anywhere near TV before. Who the hell did I think I was kidding? I read through the list again. There was nothing I wanted to cut out of it. I wanted it *all*. If Mother's magic was real, then everything on that list was going to happen.

I went back to her writings. It took me another month to read through Mother's words completely, and yet another to understand what she had written there. Dense couplets of archaic language – but once I learned to look through that, it seemed so simple how she had written it. Mother had written a spell book. Each section had a different theme – a new stage of development. Each chapter took me into a different place in myself to find out what I needed to know and, equally as important, what I needed to do to progress. Some of it I thought I knew already, but I knew it with my *head* not my *heart*. I knew it intellectually, but did not feel it – did not believe that I could make these things happen. I worked my way through the spells and incantations, through the rituals and the rites of passage from one mental space into another, until I arrived at the other end.

The first section was the traveller – the self in motion. The others form the journey. Simple. One new attitude, twelve stages to the journey and a single final destination – the Source.

Each stage had a story and a ritual connected with it. Each one was a separate lesson in itself. Each one was connected to the one before like links in a chain. Each linked to the phases of the Moon, and as she waxes and wanes, her power feeds into the Source. Waiting until the Moon is ready for you is a very important part of making your connection to the Source unforced – natural.

A number of the stages require you to go into yourself – something I had trained myself to do with hypnosis. There was no reason to wait now, I was ready to give magic a chance.

So I did just that. I worked my way through the books, trance by trance, ritual by ritual, rite by rite, and with each link in the chain got closer to my goals. By the end of eighteen months I had it all. It came as a complete shock to me. The books, the TV series, the houses, the lover. Mother had been as good as her promise. She had said that all I needed to do was to listen to her, and she would bring the magic to me. It was time to keep my promise to her, and I decided that the first book would be the one which told the world how I had transformed my life. *How To Be Amazing*. I called it. *Transform your life with hypnosis* was the subtitle. Neat, I thought. I realised that the title didn't have the word magic in it, but that wouldn't matter. People who bought it would be able to read through, and by using the self-hypnosis CD they would be able to link in with the magic. Okay, so it was my story, rather than Mother's – but I considered that most people out there would not understand if I wrote the message straight from Mother's hand. It would work better if it was my story – people would be able to relate to it and then bring magic into their lives without even knowing that was what they were doing. The book sold well. It worked for those people who read it and listened to the CD properly. Interestingly, lots of men bought it, not the usual self-help market, but I persuaded myself it was the practical style of writing that worked for them. And all the way through I convinced myself that the readers would be able to connect to the magic beneath. I had fulfilled my part of the bargain. I had shared the magic.

Blissfully happy, I worked on the TV series. As it turned out, this was a classic case of be careful what you wish for, as it wasn't the most happy experience for me. The media world is a strange one, with its own language and rituals, and to be truthful I really didn't belong. It showed me how naive I was, even though I thought I was quite streetwise. Oh no, I wasn't. Besides, the programme didn't really fit into the scheme of things for me, it was more of a modern wish – make me famous! Without actually thinking it through – especially when they changed the title at the eleventh hour to include the word 'sex'. I realised then, that I was on a runaway train. So, I took it as an interesting experience, and when people came and talked to me about other TV projects, they were genuinely surprised when I said that I wasn't all that bothered. I wasn't in that space any more. Being on TV wasn't all it was cracked up to be, and it taught me that there were layers upon layers of people who were so involved in themselves that nothing else mattered to them. There were on the other hand some truly lovely and genuine ones in that world – but they did not define themselves by their work. No surprise, they were mothers, most of them. I sometimes wondered what they would have thought if I told them that I had conjured them up from a 500-year-old spell. I am sure that some of them would not have hesitated to tell me that there was a possible series in it and that they would have their people call my people to set up a meeting. And I thought I lived in a strange world.

Filming over, I went back to work, and concentrated on my clients. At least, that was the intention. Within weeks of the programme I was paralysed with back pain. Literally. Taken to St Mary's Hospital in Paddington in an emergency ambulance, screaming my head off. Not very dignified – and completely out of the blue. I hadn't done anything to cause this as far as I knew. It was horrible. For three weeks I lay on my back unable to move. One way to test a new relationship is to be completely helpless and screaming pathetically in pain. Thankfully I had chosen well, and the relationship strengthened rather than weakened as a result. My back, however, did not, and despite any number of tests the doctors couldn't find a cause for my pain. I waited. I had a horrible feeling of foreboding that I was about to find out what this was all about.

On the twenty-first day of being imprisoned by the pain, I felt, rather than saw, her arrive. She sat on the bed and stared at me, until I closed my eyes to see her properly. *Well, well, child.* Her tone was gentle but her look was not. *You couldn't resist it, could you?* I could feel myself blushing like a ten-year-old – and behaving like one. *What do you mean?* I played for time. *The book. You couldn't just do what I asked, could you? You had to tamper and tinker with it. You had to make it* male. *You stripped out the magic and left the mechanics. You served the recipe and not the dish.* I tried to sit up to defend myself and yelped immediately, falling back onto the bed. *I put it out there – just as I had done it. I thought that was what you wanted,* I cried. *You wanted me to share it.* I could feel a tear leaking out of my eye. *I meant well. I thought that if I wrote it just as you had told it to me, then no one would want to read it. No one would believe it.*

You meant *well – listen to yourself! So you thought that people are too stupid to recognise real magic when they see it? That they wouldn't want it?* She was getting really angry now, and I did not want to be in the same room as her, but I couldn't move, couldn't get away from the growing storm of her fury. *A window had finally opened up in the mind of the populace and you refuse to acknowledge it? How many books and programmes and magazines do you see all around you with magic in them? Psychics and mediums, angel guides and tarot readers – they are everywhere! It is time to blast out the wheat from the chaff, and expose the fakes by proving that the truly magical exists within all of us. You thought you knew better!* She screamed the last phrase in true banshee style. I hid under the covers. The storm of her anger showed no signs of abating. I stayed beneath the sheets and waited.

And waited. I knew better than to try and defend myself because she was absolutely correct. I *had* tinkered. I had decided to write *my* book rather than hers. I *thought* it would get the message across more effectively. However, in my heart of hearts I knew that this was about my fear. I still could not let go of the logical male teachings which had wrapped themselves around my heart, stifling its desire for magic. I *thought* that if I put out the book in its entirety, as it had been told to me, and told precisely *how* I had got hold of this knowledge, that I would be professionally ruined. That my life as I knew it would end. All the wonderful things which I had magicked into my life would turn to dust and disappear, and I would be returned to the life from before. I was too afraid to trust the magic completely and share it with others.

The storm finally abated. I lay still on the bed, waiting. *I will write the book. I will write out all the spells just as you told them to me, and exactly as I used them. I won't mess with them in any way.* And still a part of me was saying, You do realise that people will think you have lost the plot. I tried to hide that voice from Mother but she heard it loud and clear. *Haven't you seen enough yet to trust the magic?* I stayed silent. *When you are ready to truly share with others, and not carry the whole load yourself, then your back will free itself from pain.* With that, she left. I opened my eyes and waited. I could feel no pain in my back while I lay still, and was still afraid to try and move. When eventually I plucked up the courage to try and stand, there was no pain. I sat on the edge of the bed, something I had been unable to do for weeks. No pain. I stood up shakily. No pain. I walked around the house slowly.

If you have never been in acute pain you will not understand the euphoria which I experienced that day. To be able to move around without pain was just the most incredible sensation I

had ever felt. I had no choice then. I had no choice but to keep
my promise to her. She had released me. Three weeks later,
after a number of visits to the back specialists, who still had no
idea as to what had happened to me, I was at my desk, writing.
I copied out her words, exactly as she gave them to me, and put
down how I applied her words, and what were the results in my
life. Warts and all. Funny that, when we say 'warts and all' we
mean 'with complete honesty'. Funny how artists always give
witches warts …

I digress for a moment. The truth is that there is a tiny
little part of me holding back, afraid of what I am about to
unleash. *Give over* – as Mother said to me when she spotted
this reticence. *That is your vanity gabbing, that is. You just like
the idea of being the only one with a secret. Share it or the power
within you will die … Remember, present has two meanings, the
here-and-now and gift.* That much I do know with certainty. The
power will only truly work when you share it – something that
men who have lost their connection with Mother Earth and
Sister Moon could never do. That was their undoing. Magic is
a peculiar thing. At the same time as yearning for its existence,
we take care to ignore its occurrence. Remarkable, really.
Except when you remember that we are all products of our
environment. However much we would like to think that we
are all unique and individual creatures, capable of independent
thought and action, it is, sadly, not the case. Most of us allow
ourselves to take the path of least resistance, and we end up
with an approximation of what we thought our lives were going
to contain. House, partner, job, maybe children. Holiday twice
a year if we are lucky and the prospect of getting older while we
do it. If anything out of the ordinary happens to us we either
put it down as a fluke – just luck – or we ignore it and miss an
opportunity. Unless, that is, we win the lottery.

If that happened, of course everything would be completely
different. For those people who have suddenly and unexpectedly
become rich (and I have treated a few of them professionally),

the money does not necessarily make life better. There is the knowledge that you have financial security and that you don't have to work any more if you don't want to – but with the money comes any number of unforeseen problems. Some would call them superior problems as they didn't exist before the money came along, but they are additional to, rather than replacing, any problems already in place. A bad relationship, poor mental or physical health and any number of other problems are not suddenly *fixed* by the money. They can be coped with better, of course – but not necessarily mended. Often poor relationships get worse when the money comes in because the person who is now rich is no longer prepared to work at it, and jumps into a new relationship with the same bad attitude.

In that case, what if, instead of money (and you can have that too, but we will come to that later), magic came into your life. The power to create a new life for yourself. What would be different then? From personal experience I can tell you that not everyone is ready to acknowledge even the existence of magic, let alone to realise its potential to transform lives. But let's just suspend disbelief for a moment and pretend you were prepared to become magical. What would happen? Well, first of all you would no longer be able to fool yourself into believing that there is only one version of reality – one way of doing things. You would have to take responsibility for your mistakes, your actions and start to believe in yourself and to take care of yourself better. This having been said, once you can do these things you can become a truly magical creature. The sort of person who *makes wonderful things happen*. I know. I can do this. Magic is beautiful and creative, and it is the remarkable people who walk around this earth today who do magic. These are the magnetic people, the ones you want to be around. The more of us that get involved, the more wonderful our lives become. I know what you are thinking – you want to believe, but you don't dare. You may even be afraid that people will laugh at you. This is because you live in a rational, logical world, and you have a sneaking feeling that magic is for weird people, not for successful ones. You are wrong – and I will prove it to you through the pages of this book. All you have to do is read on.

How do I define magic? The most apposite definition I have ever found is on Princeton University's website. I *love* the World Wide Web! It reads, 'Magic is any art that invokes supernatural powers.' No cloak, calling of diabolical spirits, no evil. Magic is not anti-society or anti-religion. It crosses all borders. True magic is by definition natural. Just because the word 'super' comes at the front of it does not mean it is against nature, far from it. It is an *enhancement* of that which is natural. We have been taught to fear magic because it defies description, and over the millennia anything which cannot be absorbed by organised religion or society has been destroyed by it. At least, there have been many attempts to destroy magic in its truest form, and it has always quietly reasserted itself, like a weed. Natural, strong, but men didn't cultivate it so they don't want it there and will do everything to replace, disguise or kill it if they can. It doesn't matter if that weed can heal – there are men who will still attempt to destroy its power.

And so I am writing this manual for two reasons. First, I had no choice – Mother Shipton made me! Second, because I have a gift. One which allows me to enter freely the landscape of my inner self. Maybe Mother guided me towards that too. I am not so sure about that. Either way, it was my way into being able to listen to Mother – that gift is the use of genuine trance – the real McCoy. I will show you how to control it to access your magical self, and, just as important, believe in your own potential to create magical change within and around you. By using the trance state properly you are not just going through the motions, you are connecting with your inner self in a way that will truly astound you. Entrance, *entrance* – one meaning the passageway from one space to another, and the other meaning to fill with wonder – to enchant. One word, two meanings, and in this context both meanings meet together at the doorway to your mind. For me, I use hypnosis to enter trance in a safe and controlled way. It is the doorway to my dreams. There is nothing to fear here. There are many pathways through our memories, and I will guide you through them in a way which can only enhance your life. You will be completely in control when you do this, and that control will increase as you practise mind magic.

True magic requires rites and rituals; the rites are real and are events in your daily life, the rituals are symbols of change and are meant to punctuate the rites. One before, and one after each rite. Nothing in this book is impossible or time-consuming – you can and you will do the things which will carry you to the Source *only if you choose to*. Remember, most things in life are a choice. It is just that some of us choose not to see the alternatives.

And so, here is where your story begins.

Rites, Rituals and Trances

From here on you will start to notice a sequence in the journey. You will start to work with the phases of the Moon. To fully harness the power of each phase of the Moon, the rites, rituals and trances of each chapter form a pattern – a flow. This flow is to harness the strongest energy of Sister Moon and Mother Earth. Each chapter and step on the journey links with the next phase of the Moon. You may find this gets frustrating, for the more you see magic starting to appear around and within you, and the closer you get to its Source, the quicker you will want to race on to the next phase. If you choose to do this out of sync with the lunar cycle, it is your decision – but I can tell you now that everything you do achieve will therefore be smaller than it could be. It will be pale and diminished. By rushing ahead and not waiting for the Source to grow around as well as within you, you *may* progress, but much more slowly than you would if you wait for the time to be right.

> 'To every thing there is a season, and a time to every
> purpose under the heaven'

Waiting has its place in creating change and growth. It is not all about action, but about sowing seeds of change, nurturing them, and then, when the time is right, harvesting the changes. Patience can be learned. You *will* get to the Source.

The sequence

Trance: Dark Moons
A state of heightened consciousness within which you connect with the Source and its psychic energies

Ritual: Waxing Moons
A symbolic event used here to mark the start of a process

Rite: Full Moons
An action in which you manifest in the outer world the changes taking place within you

Trance: Waning Moons
A state of heightened consciousness within which you connect with the Source and acknowledge what has passed

The meaning

Rites of passage take place at the time of the Full Moons, when the capacity for action is at its height.

Rituals take place in Waxing Moons, when you are making the preparations for change – physical, mental and spiritual.

Trances take place during the Dark Moon and Waning Moon phases of the lunar calendar. The trances in the Dark Moons harness the psychic energies there, and the Waning Moon trances bring completion and give you a chance to mourn if need be.

CHAPTER 4

Death & Dark Moon

✝

Mother writes:

Death is the start of your journey
Not the End
Only in choosing life will you become your
own friend.
Clear your path, travel light
Waste no time, uncover your light.
Hurry now, don't delay
Death will wait, whither you go – or stay.

*U*rsula Sontheil became the legend that was Mother Shipton only after she had died. For generations she was reborn in the minds of the people who had looked to her for guidance. She understood the power of belief, and that you can become anything you want by believing in yourself.

She understood that if other people believe you are capable of magic, then they are the ones who give you the power to perform it. I saw it year after year in my therapy practice. Women who were carried in, unable to stand unaided, who left my consulting room walking. I have seen tumours shrink, and anxiety and fear leave the faces of those who were too scared to leave their homes. I have shared the joy of new parents who had been told that they would never have children. I have seen many wonderful things, but know I have no more *power* than you, but what I have been given I have channelled. I know how to use it for the benefit of others. I did not make these wonderful things happen, but I did help those people find the Source of magic within *themselves* to change. That is why it was so ironic that I couldn't change myself. My life remained constrained by my own expectations. When I opened the book in which Mother Shipton had written, I found her words obscure and hard to read. So I did what I do best: I took myself into a trance, where the words became pictures, and the pictures became a story – a journey. The story became clear and simple to me. I imagined what it would be like for me to die, to leave this life and all the things which I should have done but didn't. It helped me decide that it was time to start living before I died. I visualised my own funeral. It was a cold and unfriendly affair. The eulogy talked of my work, and the people whom I had helped professionally, but there was no one there to mourn me. People seemed sad, but I had not touched any one person in real depth – with meaning. I felt cold and isolated as I watched this, and angry that I had allowed my life to become so empty of meaning. I realised (and it made me smile in a strange sort of way) that I wanted weeping, wailing and gnashing of teeth. I wanted music and laughter and a party with those who loved me to celebrate my life. I wanted *more* from my death, just as I now wanted more from my life. I cried tears of regret and self-pity, anger and frustration. I mourned the passing of someone now dead to me. I finally registered that it is the awareness of our own death, our absolute mortality that is essential to living life to the full – every moment of it. For years I had seen clients with cancer, and saw the pure shining glow of life in their eyes. They all knew what most of us choose not to register, and that is the essential fact that life is for living *now* – not tomorrow, or next week, but today. Right here, right now is where life begins. I grew thankful that I had learned this while there was still time to change the future.

When I woke from my trance, I pulled out my notebook and began to write down all the things I had regretted not doing, all the feelings which came to me, and added it to the list of the things which I had already written down and I now wanted to do more than ever. I let the trance continue into my writing, and I did not restrict myself. I felt more alive even than on the mountain. Now I was becoming *hungry*, hungry for life. Hungry for the fulfilment of my dreams and hopes, the things which inspired me and made me eager for more life. I took time over this — and I would ask you to do the same. The easiest way to do this is to ask your unconscious awareness to give you this information. It may be that some of these dreams and desires are still hidden from you. Take yourself into your own inner world. Trance comes naturally to each of us every day when we daydream, but more significantly it comes to us easily in the moments between waking and sleeping.

So this is what you need to do to experience this. Just before going to sleep tonight, lie down in your bed with your eyes closed and count down from 300 to zero. Do this in complete darkness. Use your out breath to time the numbers, and when you reach zero you will be connecting to your inner world. There is nothing to fear here, but if you find your heart beating faster recognise that this is the life force within you, and it may not appreciate or understand what you are doing. It is time to then imagine what it would be like to leave the life you are living — as if you were actually dying. You can feel yourself leaving your body, see your own funeral, and move among the mourners like a ghost. You will then become aware of all the things you wish you had said and done. This is the time when all your regrets will come to you, and you will know what it is you need to focus on changing. You may feel the need to cry — to mourn. Let it happen. It is understandable and natural. When you have finished, you can rest a moment and think about this experience. Then open your special book, take your pen and start writing. Write down your hopes and dreams, your regrets and wishes. Take time over this. There may be more things you want to write down than you would have expected. Don't censor yourself, just write everything that comes into your mind. You can now prepare yourself to sleep normally.

If you do not feel comfortable doing this, when you come to the trance sections in later chapters, just imagine yourself on the journeys which I will describe for you to take. Everyone experiences trance in the way in which they feel most safe. You are in control throughout this process and there is no one right way to experience this – only your way.

Once I had written all my dreams and desires, I went back to Mother Shipton's writings.

Mother writes:

Before taking each step, cleanse yourself with water
   and words.
Fill your bowl and rinse your hands
As you rub your hands together, say:
'I cleanse myself for the next step
What went before leaves me and joins the sea'
Do this thrice then wipe and hide your bowl.

I cleansed myself, and now it was time for the next step.

Having looked at my life as if it were over, it was now time **to clear out everything that had belonged to the woman I no longer wanted to be.** I was getting a chance to leave one life while still alive and make another. Clothes and shoes were easy. I cleared out the kitchen cupboards, I cleared out the spare-room wardrobes, I cleared out the attic. Boxes and boxes of *things*. Don't get me wrong, I like possessions, and I especially like *nice* things. But I had far too much. I took bags and bags to the charity shop, I sold things on eBay, I gave books away to my friends.

I pared back on everything I owned. I had to. I knew that the next stage in the journey was that of the traveller and that travellers move best when they travel light. No point in excess baggage, it will only slow you down.

I kept my Vivienne Westwood suit, though, because I knew I would need it for a little longer, until I was safe in my transformation. I knew that I wouldn't need it for much longer though. I was sure I wouldn't go back to that life. Mother's final words to me – *present has two meanings, the here-and-now and gift* – had stuck in my mind. There was no time like the present to get on and begin anew and make the present my gift to myself.

And so, from here on in, this book becomes a handbook, a manual, albeit one illustrated by the example of my change. As with many handbooks, you will need some basic equipment. This is for the rituals themselves. All true magic is about rites and rituals. The rites are real and are events in your daily life, the rituals are symbols of change and are meant to punctuate the rites. Nothing in this book is impossible or time-consuming – you can and you will do the things which will carry you to the Source *only if you choose to go there*. The journey creates the magic, and when complete it will never leave you. Remember – most things in life are a choice – it is just that some of us choose not to see the alternatives.

You will need the following:

Fire (candle)
Air (outdoors or a room with an open window)
Earth (barefoot is best)
Water (a small fireproof bowl)
A notebook, some loose-leaf paper and a special pen
    (only for magic)

Finally, when selecting your tools, remember that the appreciation of beauty is also a part of true magic, so when you choose items that are going to become part of your magic rituals, keep this in mind.

So you have started the journey with your death, and can now cleanse yourself with water and Mother's words – *before taking each step*. You are ready to start in earnest now. So here you are. Take a deep breath. There is nothing difficult or complicated here. The rituals are simple. One to start each process, and one to end it. Nothing more. I will take you through what to do with each one carefully at the relevant times. As well as your equipment you need a space in which to do the ritual. Some people go into the garden, some create a space in their bedroom, others go out deep into nature. If it is your space, keep it clean and tidy. If you work in nature, clear a small area. Find a space to hide your notebook, candle and other equipment, somewhere safe and known only to you, and do not use them for any other purpose. I decided to create my own candle, blended with frankincense to increase determination, and almonds to encourage money and luck. I called it *Success* and on the day I married I filled the room where the ceremony took place with the light from this candle. Every time I smell that combination it gives me joy and I connect with that day, knowing that I am capable of making magic real in my life.

Secrecy, too, is part of magic, and do not underestimate its potency. You can keep your rituals secret (and safe) by opening a circle before and closing it afterwards. Before each ritual the circle is opened. This action is to reinforce the fact that you are preparing a special space in which to act. This space is pure of any other thought or action, and you dedicate the time in the circle to opening up your connection with the Source. You make space for magic in your life.

What is the circle? The circle is a protected area in which you perform rituals. Within the circle you communicate directly with the Source. You open and close the circle to create a space in which you can safely access the Source, and nurture and protect it. It is important that you value it and measure out its use. Never waste it or it will diminish. Think of it as a light which needs fuel. Nourish the Source and it will nourish you. As you get closer to the end of the journey, the strength of the Source will grow, as will your recognition of it as a force.

Why does the circle need to be opened and closed? The Source needs to remain contained and concentrated. When you open the circle, it is similar to opening a door to enter a room. Until the door is open you remain on the outside. Closing the circle when your ritual is over protects the Source and prevents it from 'leaking away'. If you do not close the circle you open yourself up to letting randomness enter your daily life. This is not a good idea. It can be very exciting and stimulating, but you have no control over it. The Source in itself is not malicious, or indeed emotional in any way, but it is an energy – and if you leave a door open for it to roam, it will do just that. Closing the circle is also a sign of recognition that the Source exists in relation to you and no other.

How to open and close the circle

Traditionally the circle is opened by walking around the space three times in a clockwise direction. Closing the circle is the reverse, walking anticlockwise or widdershins as it is sometimes called. You can also do this by closing your eyes and mentally walking the space, or if you have access to a space open to the sky, you can sweep the circle with a broom, either by contact with the earth, or sweeping the sky by raising the broom above your head. Or you can do this by visualising a circle of light moving around the space. The final way is to do this with sound – chanting, humming or singing to define a circle around you. You can even find your own way if you wish. The only thing of importance is that whatever you do to open the circle, you reverse the action to close it. This way you maintain a safe psychic space in which to operate, and it stays outside your 'normal' time and ways of thinking.

You will also need to learn with whom it is safe to share your knowledge of the Source and to avoid contact with those who have lived their lives too long in the Dark Moon. The Journey will help you with this. Remember, Luna creates her own form of madness for those sucked into her depth, those who hand over their power to her and expect her to create on their behalf. You will quickly recognise who these people are, and how to protect yourself from their simple madness.

Another component in the magic will be in learning to recognise and tune into your natural rhythms, and to those of nature itself. Connecting with nature in a way that is practical and accessible for you is an important factor in creating magic in your life, and in ensuring that you work with nature rather than against it. Even in a city we can connect with the natural around and within us. All this will be part of the process. And you know, the most magical part of it all is just how natural this will feel to you. When you connect with your inner magic and project it outwards you will feel extraordinary – supernatural – and so you will be. Embrace it – the magic you have waited for all this time is here in these pages, ready and waiting to come into your life.

Now you are newly born, you can start familiarising yourself with the rites and rituals of passage from darkness to the Source, and from here on in, each chapter will take you through a commencement ritual, a rite of passage, and a closure ritual. Each chapter has either a trance experience, a ritual to build into your life, or an event forming a rite of passage. The chapters have a flow from one to the other – a rhythm. The chapters breathe the Source into you with each trance, and remove the external obstacles to change in the rite-of-passage chapters. You can move through each of the chapters in time with the Moon phases, harnessing the energy of Luna with each step of your transformation, or you can read straight through and work on the rites and rituals when the Moon phases come round. It is your journey to the Source – not mine, and you will choose your route based on your knowledge of yourself. However, never forget how long it took you to get to this stage. Perhaps a little patience is part of your learning. There will also be times when you feel frustrated, and just want to get on to the next stage – the next chapter, but you will find that waiting is part of the preparation, ensuring you will be ready for the next step towards the Source of true magic.

The rituals will show that you are preparing yourself for each step, opening you up to action. When you have completed each rite of passage – each action, you are giving thanks. Rituals are very important, and sadly most of us have lost our connection to the Source because we do not have time. Or so we say, so we would rather believe. The fact is that by allowing the rituals to fade from our lives we have weakened the connections between our rich inner world and the outer world – we have lost much of our connection to the Source. By taking time to do each ritual, and by focusing on it and nothing else, you are once again opening up the door between the two worlds. In doing so you will change reality – you can truly do magic. You can heal yourself and the world, one step at a time.

I will illustrate each step of the inner journey with my own journey through each stage. Before, you were led by me, from now on it is time for you to travel alongside me, guided by Mother and those others who have trodden the path to the Source.

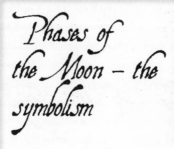

Dark Moon

The Dark Moon follows the Waning Moon and is linked to the energies of the Crone figure. The dark moon sits on the cusp of destruction and creation, and her power is volatile. The Dark Moon is said to be linked to lunacy as a Dark Moon can deceive. It is the absence from which all things can be created – a universal blank page.

Remember this is a time when the tides recede furthest from the shore, and with this they leave so much exposed. The Dark Moon is both the moon of illusion and powerful psychic connection, so you need to be strong to work with this lunar phase.

The Dark Moon symbolises the wisdom of experience and age, and is a time when it is good to become aware of the games which you play on yourself, and free yourself from the illusions created by you as a result. No one can trick or fool you but you – and if you try to hold on to an illusion in the light of the Dark Moon, then you can go crazy with the effort.

Let go of your games, your tricks and your illusions at this time. It may mean letting go of a long-held belief about yourself, or the people or world around you.

It is a time of grieving as well as a time of relief. You can let go of your grief of personal loss at this time, and be liberated by the process.

CHAPTER 5

Preparing for the Journey Find Your Light – Waxing Moon

||||

Ritual

It is time to familiarise yourself with the phases of the Moon and the power of waking to the Sun. Time also to include rituals into your life and understand their importance. Rituals focus the mind. They can be repeated until they become a pattern without conscious thought. Through the patterns of rituals you will start to link to the patterns of the Moon, and through her you will connect with the patterns around you. Everything you need to become magical is already here – surrounding you. You just need to recognise the patterns. It may seem unstructured and chaotic to you now, but deep in the chaos is the pattern for magic. The route to the Source.

Rituals run deep through our psyche. When you perform a ritual you are giving something of yourself to the Source. You step out of your daily life and you connect – however briefly – with something greater than yourself. Rituals soothe the mind and help you to let go of irritations and frustrations. The rituals in this book are described to you, but you do not need to do them exactly as set out. They are not *prescribed*, but guidelines. Magic is something you will create for yourself, and that also means performing rituals which feel right to you. By all means, do them as I have written them if you feel comfortable to do so, but if you want to adapt them to incorporate personal beliefs, please do. The Wyrd* Web survives because it is flexible, and you will learn how to be flexible with your rituals, rites of passage and your trances once the journey of this book is over. Once completed, you will continue with your own variations. You will be the author of your own magical destiny and the rites, rituals and trances which you perform as part of this journey. More of that later. Just remember at this point if you are confused, it is good. The experience of chaos is part of the Source itself. Nothing is meant to stay the same. You will learn how to accept and to create change to derive magical patterns from the chaos around and within. No need to try. It will come to you. Just read on.

Mother writes:

Circles within, circles without,
Patterns thrice wove are swiftly sans doubt.
Link tightly with Luna and your rituals take shape.
Ignore her time and your connection abates.

Someone once said to me when I complained that I didn't have time to write a book, 'Do you know how old you'll be when you've written your book? The same age you would be if the book hadn't been started.' There was never going to be time to write unless I made it a priority. So I did. I started writing. Three

---

* Wyrd – Anglo-Saxon word meaning destiny. One of the three sisters of Fate.

hundred and fifty words a day. I decided my first book was going to be 40,000 words. So if I wrote 350 words a day – around a page of text – and I wrote five days a week with weekends off, then I would complete the book in around 115 days. That would be around twenty-three weeks, or six months. I could get up an hour earlier every day, and write 350 words, couldn't I? Yes, I could, and yes, I did. In fact the hardest part was stopping every day. I found myself sneaking in another couple of hundred words whenever I could. Each day, before I ate or showered, I would write. In the peace of the early morning before the London streets awoke I formed words of power. I did this until the diggers and police sirens formed the soundscape of my city and the outside world moved closer. I had created a ritual. A pattern that I would repeat until it became automatic. Out of the chaos in my life I created a pattern. A small one at first, but one which I soon found reflected above and below me as I started to believe. I wrote daily. Without thought or pause. It was my first ritual. I started to trust.

In writing a book I had to seek and find a light to guide me – to keep the ritual alive. You must find your own light within you. This light will illuminate your path to the Source. You must nurture your light. What is the one thing that you want to do above all others? What is your dream? To write a book, to paint a picture, to start a business, find your life partner, heal a rift with your family, to help others? Uncover the one thing above all others which you regretted not doing when you took yourself to your own death, and then clear your path. You may have no really clear idea of what it is that will become your light, but this chapter will help you open yourself up to the direction from which it will come to you. From the darkness of your death you will move towards your light, and by being true to yourself you will begin to trust its echo within you. By connecting with nature and her rituals you will tune into the light around you, and by connecting to the Source you will achieve your dreams and more. Oh, and while we're not on the subject, **get rid of**

those possessions which are dragging you down. Do you really *need* the exercise bike in the garage? *Get rid of it!* Sell it and put the money into the dream fund. Act as if the person who you were when you bought them is now gone. You have no further use for these specific possessions, no matter who gave them to you or how much they cost. If you spend more time cleaning or rearranging a possession than using or appreciating it, or if it is stuck away in a place where you cannot even get to it – it's time to let it go. Time to travel *light*.

The relief you'll experience is incredible. Once you start this clearing process you have no choice but to continue. It took several months to get to the stage where the only things in my home were either beautiful or useful. No more stuffed drawers, or clothes hidden away in the back of the wardrobe. I cleared out my papers as if in preparation for my death, but I knew that in doing this I was preparing for life. So much bad karma shredded and sent to be recycled into toilet paper. It seems so right, somehow.

To start *any* journey you need to prepare. This is what you are doing now in taking control of the things which surround you, and once defined you. You are preparing for your new life. Talk to anyone who has lost most of their possessions in a fire or a flood – they will tell you that almost all had no meaning. They only regretted losing photographs or other items of great sentimental value. Sometimes the pleasure gained from giving things to those who will value them more than you can be immeasurable. These are the moments which will give you the gentle nudges to let you know that what you are doing is okay.

So, how to contact the light? Simple, really. Draw back the curtain. For deep in your brain is an area called the pineal gland. This is your light sensor, known as the master gland or the third eye. Over the centuries it has been attributed with metaphysical as well as physical properties. René Descartes called it the 'seat of the soul'. For you, it will be the pathway to your inner light. To activate it, start to make a habit of sensing the daylight before you open your eyes each morning. Allow yourself to wake naturally to the daylight rather than to the sound of an alarm clock jarring you out of your sleep. By leaving a curtain partly open you will let nature wake you to the light, and by allowing yourself to sense this light before your eyes open each day, you create an awareness of those things around you which will awaken the light within. By connecting with nature your inner light will start to respond to the world around you – making connections which you would *never* have seen without allowing nature to stimulate the deeper workings of your brain. Do not underestimate this connection, and do not *try* to make it happen. Just let it happen – allow yourself to awaken to daylight. You will begin to notice as you start to wake naturally that you wake more gently, and you spend longer in the state between waking and sleeping – in DreamTime – where your inspiration exists and your dreams take shape ready for reality. This is natural trance. **Make the connection daily and when you have finished and are ready for the day, write down the thoughts which came to you in your special book. Write down what you want from the day, and do not censor your words.** You may also find that a new inner voice – that of your guide – starts to come to you unasked for while you are in DreamTime. Don't worry if it doesn't happen, there is a specific step on the journey to help you find and connect with your guide.

With the knowledge of the light came awareness of the darkness and a need to know the lunar agenda so I put a widget of Moon phases on my iPhone*. If I was going to make this magic work I would have to work with all Mother Earth and Sister Moon had to offer me, and connecting my rites, rituals and trances to the lunar phases would amplify them. Mother told me and I listened. I did not always enjoy having to wait to

---

* iPhemeris

complete the steps to the Source, but by now I was starting to trust. If you want to experience this journey fully you will need to familiarise yourself with the phases of the Moon. You can find a lunar calendar that will sit on your computer desktop, or there are paper diaries with the lunar phases marked in them.

I now had my lunar clock, and as per Mother's instructions I was going to work in time with that clock. It was to be my timetable along the journey to the Source. I was waking to the light, so I needed to become aware of the patterns of the dark hours, just as you will if you really want to work with nature and connect to the Source of true magic. My first stage on the journey was to be during the Waxing Moon. A preparation Moon. Working with the Waxing Moon gave the clearing a purpose. I wasn't getting rid of possessions, I was preparing for freedom. At first I couldn't tell whether I found this so easy because I had to wait for the moon to enter a Waxing phase, or in waiting I became impatient to get rid of things so I could get started. I could feel my enthusiasm for the journey rising within me. What I can say is that once I had cleared out my physical space it really highlighted my need to evaluate my emotional space. I was holding on to my ideas and feelings with as much tenacity – if not more – as I had held on to my possessions. My preparation for the journey took place in the light of the Waxing Moon, and I started to feel the magic growing inside me. I was beginning to get excited. The lunar phase for preparation was amplifying my desire and readiness to create change in my life, and to find my way to the Source.

There is nothing to stop you, of course, doing the rituals, rites and trances as and when you want to – but remember, to harness the power of the Source you need to work with what is around you as well as the drive within you. Better to wait for the energy of Sister Moon to give the rituals and rites true potency. You have waited this long to connect to the Source, a few more weeks one way or another won't matter.

As much as my physical space had become cluttered and unmanageable, so had my mental space. I had become afraid of doing nothing – because if I was doing nothing then I might have to start thinking. I knew – *we all know* – the thoughts and feelings which give us the most grief. **Take individual sheets of paper and get your special pen out. Write down all the feelings which you believe have held you back. Put each on an individual page and spread them out in front of you, study them as if these emotions belong to a dead you – a you who no longer exists.** A you who died without doing anything to change these feelings. What is there in your heart – resentment, anger, frustration? Spread them all out onto separate pages. Each one of these emotions will form the basis of a task for you to fulfil. A task which will free yourself from these feelings – you will be born anew with only the emotions you want. You will have identified the first part of your path to the Source – the obstacles – and you will now start clearing them so your journey can be smooth. You are on your way.

For me, the emotions were unedifying. Anger, resentment, jealousy, a sense of moral and intellectual superiority, irritation at others, arrogance, greed … I filled up quite a few sheets of paper. I didn't like what I found within myself, and nor will you. **For, as you progress on your journey to the Source, you will be able to remove each sheet of paper, one by one – and ritually burn it.** When you have completed a rite of passage for each, you will finalise it with a ritual so there is no way that this emotion can find its way back into your life. You will be free from the burden of that emotion. You will know when each page is ready for the fire. You are now about to set off on your journey to the Source of your own magic.

CHAPTER 6

A Traveller – Full Moon

####

Rite

Mother writes:

The traveller's blind who sees no past
Eyes on the future, his path binds fast.
Step off his path and then you might
Be guided by thine own true light.

Commencement Rite

Walk around your home. Go to every room. Open all the cupboards and the drawers. Go into the spaces you normally never go to. Pay attention to everything you see there. Now go for a walk outside and try to recall everything you have seen. What really registered? Photographs, mementos? What would you actually rescue if there was a fire? What about everything else? Do you really need all that *stuff*? Think about it. What *really* matters to you?

In the classic images of the tarot, the traveller is depicted in motion, moving away from the viewer. The tarot's traveller is male and carries a small light bundle in one hand, containing all of his worldly goods. In the other he carries a light – a light he stares blindly into. At his heels is a dog representing the past, jumping up – but the traveller pays no attention. The tarot's male traveller is a feckless wanderer, known as the fool, periodically showing up in the pack again as a magician – a manipulator. Your journey to the Source has started, but you are a fool no longer, nor will you be satisfied to tread the blind path of a fool any more. It is a fool who blindly accepts their current situation as the only reality – and by starting on this journey you have shown yourself to be different from the fool. You already recognise that there is more to reality than simply what your senses choose to register around you. You are not like the cards' magician, either, as your magic will not be of tricks and fakery – but of changing perception and shifting reality. Your magic will be truly supernatural, rather than a pale imitation. This magic can be high or low. You get to choose.

The traveller you are about to become is very different from anything you have known before. To start with you do not need to physically *go* anywhere to find the Source. The world is full of books about journeys to Tibetan temples, or Egyptian tombs, or Mayan lines, where travellers go to discover themselves. Your journey starts and ends within the self, and the first lesson of the traveller is to recognise that you can create a whole new, wonderful world within you that will arrange itself around you too – in the space you inhabit now. Hold on to the thought that the Source is already so close to you, you can almost touch it. It is real. It is within you.

Close your eyes for a moment. Take three deep breaths. Think about your life now. What do you notice when you do this? Do you feel anger, frustration, pain, sadness or nothing at all? Do you feel excited about the life you currently have? You should. You will . . .

Each negative emotion you hold on to acts as a veil hiding the Source from you. As you progress on this journey and free yourself of each of these feelings, the Source moves ever closer and you will feel its presence moving into your daily life.

And so to move on. Once you have cleared your physical space, wait for the next Waning Moon and this will be the time for you to gently ease yourself into thinking differently about who you are and how you define yourself. Always keep in the back of your mind that the physical and emotional clearing process is about the end of the old you. As such this may also be a time of regret and reflection, a time when you look back on your life up until this point, and feel sad or emotional about some events, or people. It is needed so that you can recognise where and who you are now. But, unlike death of the flesh, this is a phoenix death, one from which you will be reborn, renewed. Just like Alfred Nobel,* you will be given the chance to live a new life, and have a different death. Nobel managed this when his death was erroneously reported. 'Dr Death is dead,' said the newspapers. With this wake-up call as to what people thought of him, Nobel thereby got a chance to reflect on his life and his inventions, and decided there and then that he would change his future. He set up the Nobel prizes, and remarkable people have done some incredible things in earning these prizes. When Nobel actually died, he was remembered for the Nobel peace prize above all others. He was no longer Dr Death.

Right now, you have the opportunity to look back on your life so far and make change happen – to experience a metaphorical death and to be reborn as you wish to become. As Mother and her knowledge moves to the periphery of your senses, you can now start to imagine what life could be like if you are strong enough to follow your senses, to trust your instinct on the way to the Source and to allow magic into your life. Rather than hating and hiding the selves which you exposed in your sheets,

* The inventor of dynamite.

the start of your journey is to confront them, and in doing so, free yourself of them.

For each of those negative selves, there is a task. To free yourself from your past you will take those pages on which you have written the emotions, and choose which you will confront first. Take the simplest. Make it easy on yourself – not like I did. I jumped in both feet first thinking that by tackling the most difficult I would show that I was strong. No need. Take the easiest and learn. No need to force the process because the opportunities to free yourself will come to you. For me, I chose to deal with my jealousy first.

What and who was I jealous of? I was jealous of those whom I thought had advanced in my profession, because I believed I was better than them. I was jealous of those who seemed to sail through life without effort or strain. I was jealous of so many other people. I was jealous of those who had been born with more opportunities than me, and most of all those who had been born with advantages and had chosen not to use them. I had a sizeable list of individuals and types of people whom I had chosen to make into my enemy. The thing is, when you evaluate each of your demons (because that is precisely what you are doing here), you will find there may be many sub-sections, some of which you hadn't even thought about until you turned your attention to them. **Write down whatever occurs to you on the back of the relevant sheet.** Put it all down. As you do, you will find something starts to happen to you – you realise that it is all so pointless, and ultimately exhausting.

There will always be people in the world who have something which you do not, something of which you can be jealous *if you choose to let this happen to you*. I recognised that the damage done is by you to you. Studies in epigenetics have proven this. Emotional pain and stress ages you, makes you ill, it can ultimately even kill. And all the while the people of whom I was jealous didn't even know how I felt – in some cases didn't even know I existed. So I let it go. Not only mentally, **but by choosing to act generously to one of those people who had**

stimulated my jealousy. This was to be my rite of passage. My way of freeing myself from this worm of jealousy. I gave one particular person something which I possessed and they wanted – in this case it was information – something which I knew they could use to become even more successful and potentially give me even more reason to be jealous. I gave it to them freely – and it was me who was liberated by the act. I realised that all the jealousy I had been storing up inside myself was preventing me from doing the very thing I envied the other person for. My jealousy was holding back my professional success. I was too busy looking at their success to attend to my own. It was a moment of revelation for me, and Mother guided me through each action I took to free myself from the demons of my past.

Jealousy can take many forms. Some years ago, I married for the first time. This was after twelve years of living with my partner. I wanted security, I wanted marriage and, most of all, I wanted a child. I wanted more than he was able to give me, and maybe some part of me knew that, but we married anyway. I wanted to move away from the party life which we had together, which was full of noise and people. He feared the silence – so did I. He bought me a rocking chair and I imagined myself holding my child, soothing the baby with its motion. We married in Las Vegas, slap bang in the middle of the porn oscars. To cap it all we were propositioned by a couple of the winners on our wedding night. Perhaps I should have read this as an omen that things were not going to go according to my plans. Real classy – what can I say – but it was a real wedding, a legally binding marriage. Reality set in for me three bloodied months later when I mourned my empty womb. No child. The rocking chair sat empty and accusingly still. The baby I had dreamed of holding in my arms grew paler and less distinct with each passing month and my husband and I grew apart and let the deafening silence build a wall between us. I moved closer into my working life and further and further away from him.

The noise returned to our lives, and it seemed back to the

old normal for a while. Then a few weeks later my husband announced that he was in love with another woman. He cried enough tears for both of us and then asked my advice. I gave it to him in a cool, professional manner. I wasn't there any more – do you understand? I had a choice to make then. How would I choose to react to her? I could poison myself with jealousy and hate and lash out at the world, or I could find my own space in this rearrangement of my life. This woman asked to meet me. She wanted to meet me to apologise because she didn't even know I existed when she got into the relationship with my husband. I thought her either brave or crazy, but in the end I agreed to meet her. She was young, beautiful, alone and in a foreign country. I no longer had a choice. My 'enemy' had a face and emotions and because of this I could not hate. Others around me encouraged me to go down the route of my head – to do the mindless thing and hate her unconditionally, but it just didn't feel right any more. I decided to listen to my heart, or at least to listen to the voice of the mother in me that now would never be. I wanted to forgive. So I did. We became friends. Close friends. They got married. In less than a year he fell in love yet again – this time with an even younger version. I had a choice to make once more. I could either crow and celebrate the fact that what had happened to me had also happened to her, or I could support her. We moved in together. I chose to support her, and she supported me in return. In this woman I now have a sister. When she divorced we went to the Thames to complete a ritual together. We waited until Big Ben chimed midday, and together we threw our wedding rings into the river. Water carried away our bonds from him, and forged the bond with one another.

She is part of my life now and will be for a long time. Mother knew what she was doing when she brought her to me. She bore the same name as the tombstone under which Mother's bones were laid to rest by Toby.* She is part of my karmic journey, I

* Mother Shipton's husband.

suppose. When life surprises you, do not do what you think you *ought* to do – do what your heart tells you, what you would wish on yourself in that situation. This will free you to become at one with the Source. You become powerful and magical by these actions – you just don't know it yet. It seems hard right now to know how all of this fits into getting the life you want, to making your own life magical. Stay with me. I cannot say this enough – it doesn't matter *who* is right, but *what* is right. It *will* make sense. The magic is working its way into your life even as you read these words. Listen to the voice within, your instinct – this one has the power. The voice without, those people who will tell you what to do when problems occur, those who say 'You ought to ...' Don't listen to them. You know better than that. You know how to heal yourself – by treating the other as you would have others treat you. **Give your time, your compassion, and your love to others and it will come back to you amplified many times.** I don't just believe it, I know it, because I have seen it for myself.

Who was there to forgive? Was there anyone who had set out to hurt me in all of this? It wasn't about me. I stepped out of my egotistical need to feel it was personal, and recognise that my pain was collateral damage in this event, and that there were three people in pain when this happened. I forgave all of them, including myself. That is the thing, you see. When you forgive, sometimes you forget that you need forgiving for your part in the event. I took responsibility for sticking my head in the sand and escaping headlong into my work when I should have been minding my own life better. I took responsibility and I forgave myself. Understand that you do not need someone else to forgive you – but you must, must forgive yourself because in doing so you take responsibility for your role, and if you need to, you must atone for your actions – *and then you can move on.* The Source will provide the ability for you to forgive. It will come sooner than you think, don't try to force it. Forgiveness liberates you from guilt and anger, and it frees you from the cycle of darkness. Most important of all, forgiveness allows you to accept magic into your life when it comes along, instead of putting out the fire and stamping on the ashes of your own happiness. You will be able to accept synchronous happenings, good experiences and happy times without the feeling that you do not deserve them (as you may have done in the past). Forgiveness lifts one of the veils and you will see life more clearly.

Mother writes:

When Moses had to stay his hand,
Joshua and Caleb brought fruit from the Promised
  Land
Find your faith and know your mind,
Your guiding light you have yet to find.
Your light is within, tho' you be yet blind.

Completion Ritual

When the Moon wanes, go out of doors into the garden if you can. If you cannot find a space in the open where you can be private, open the window of your room wide and let the air into your space. Open the circle, light the candle, and watch the air move the candle flame around. Close your eyes and allow a negative colour to come into your mind to represent the emotion which you most want to release. Breathe in this colour. Allow it to fill you completely. Let yourself experience the feeling as much as you possibly can. Allow memories and thoughts to come to you in which you feel this negative strongly. Do this for as long as you can tolerate it. Now open your eyes for a moment and focus once more on the light of the flame. Watch it for a few moments until you hold the image in your mind, then close your eyes again and see the imprint of the flame on your mind's eye. Now imagine you are breathing the dark colour out, and it is being carried away by the air around you. You can now breathe in the essence of the flame. The light of the Source. Keep doing this until all of the colour of your negative emotion is wiped clean from you by the light of the flame.

Open your eyes and rest for a moment, before putting out the candle and closing the circle. In your own way, thank the air for cleansing you. Close the window, or return indoors.

Samhain

This festival begins at the end of October in the north-ern hemisphere, and at the end of April in the southern. Samhain has links with Halloween, the day of the dead, or All Saints and All Souls, and is the time when the veil between that which lives and the dead is at its most thin. It is a powerful time to connect with members of our family or close friends who have died and to give them life once more with your stories of them. It is a time to tell tales of the dead and rejoice in the gifts they gave you, in the lives they led. It is a time to respect those no longer living, and to make decisions about how you live your life, and to call on the wisdom of those who lived before to guide you in the decisions you are about to make.

This time celebrates the end of the harvest, the start of winter and the shift from light to dark, and it marks the beginning of the Celtic new year, so it is also celebrated as a time of rebirth. Above all it is a celebration of the dark and is the counterbalance to Beltane, the festival of spring and light.

To Wiccans this is the most significant of the Greater Sabbats, as it is seen as the start of the new year as well as the beginning of winter, the dark time of the year.

It is a time when bonfires are lit, and the future can be seen for those who know how to look. It is a time to put on masks, and be as another. The rituals associated with Samhain revolve around honouring ancestors, letting go of the past and foreseeing the future.

At Samhain you can allow yourself to connect with your own personal history, and reflect on the events that have brought you to this time. It is a time to strengthen yourself by recognising and working on personal weakness-es as you move into winter, when you need to be strong.

CHAPTER 7

The New Born – Waning Moon

||||

Trance

Mother writes:

Mewling and whelping are you born
Helpless and blind
Mother cares for you
Mother feeds you
Mother teaches you
Every single day you are born anew

Commencement Ritual

The newborn has to learn how to stand on its own two feet before it can walk, and keep at it until it can walk unaided.

For you every day from now on, while you find your path to the Source, tread a path out in the world. Experiences will come to you unbidden when you are open to them. The most important thing is to get out into the air and walk. Communicate with the world around you, however unnatural it feels at first.

And before you tell me you do not have time, you can find time in the day to walk for ten minutes, can't you? For like the newborn you need to learn how to walk — but this time *mindfully*. Walking now has new meaning for you, as when you walk you can enter a trance — a walking meditation if you will. When you walk, your connections to the Source will be reinforced. You will grow in strength and stamina for the road ahead. Observe your surroundings, the signs and sounds, the smells and the feelings which being out of doors instils in you.

For now that you have taken the first step of the traveller on your journey to the Source, and packed your bags for the inner journey, there is no going back, and you will need stamina to make it all the way. You are now a traveller with a purpose, with everything you need to hand. You have rid yourself of excess baggage and can travel light — and more importantly you can respond quickly to change. It is natural that your first steps will be wobbly and unsure. You won't get every rite right, but it doesn't really matter. It is the intention not the form that matters. You will find your own and better way of doing these things. My words are only there to guide you. You will find within each rite of passage a natural progression, and even when things do not seem to go according to your original plan, understand that in the scheme of the journey it has actually worked out fine. Let it go and move on. You are the newborn who needs support and attention. It is for you to realise that the only person who can give you this support and attention is yourself — and, for now, Mother. There will be others of the Moon who will come into your life and walk alongside you for part of the journey, and you will support each other, and your guide will join you for some of the steps along the way — but only when you ask them, and they will only come to you when you actually *need* them. You cannot demand their presence. No one individual will be with you for the whole journey. You are born alone, and you will reach your destination alone. Learn this now, and learn it well.

We each have our own journey, our own path to find and

tread. The road is not a direct one, and there are times when you may be frustrated that it seems to lead you away from your goal. Accept it. Appreciate the journey. Life being what it is, you may find that you choose to spend some time on another's path, supporting them, learning from them or being their guide, but understand and remember well that their path to success is not yours, and you cannot claim their journey as your own, just as you cannot and must not claim their success as yours. I know. Petty jealousy and envy of those whom I have taught and guided became a poison in my old life – a poison that prevented me from moving forward. At the time I didn't realise it. I believed that those whom I had helped should acknowledge my part in their success. I grew bitter and petty. Mother taught me that the only way to progress on the path to success is to relinquish all claims on those you have helped.

In my past life (as I now refer to it) it was as if I had an inbuilt emotional scale, and could tell you down to the ounce who 'owed' me. As it was, I was the one weighed down with the burden of debt, wondering when they were going to pay me back, and how. Mother taught me to recognise that my gifts to others were just that – gifts – not loans. There should never have been strings attached from my side. They became the ties that bound me. I had to learn that sometimes there was never going to be any payback, at least not from the person themselves. You need to learn this lesson over and above all the others – give freely and with love. Only when you do this will you administer the antidote to the poison of jealousy and envy. I found this hard, very hard, but once I had done it I created emotional space in myself to give *more*, but in a way that replenished me, rather than diminished my sense of who I am and what I am capable of.

How do you make this happen? You will experience a similar process as before, when you visualised your death. From here on, when you come to these trance sections, this is where you cannot help but become part of the journey. You will participate in this as much or as little as you need, but remember even if all you do is read the trances, you will still relive them in your dreamscape at night. You are becoming the traveller, just as I did.

Just before going to sleep tonight, enter your trance by counting down from 300 to zero, using your out breath to time each number as you count down. If you prefer to just imagine yourself walking through this experience, the choice is yours. Either way, you will find that this process gets easier to do each time you do it. This time, when you reach zero, or you are ready to do so, just imagine yourself picking up a large sack. The sack is full to the top with smaller bags. In each small bag is a weight. Each weight is formed from a negative feeling or thought which you have been carrying with you through your life. No need to know specifically what these things are, but you know they are heavy. As you count down, imagine yourself trying to walk down some steps. The steps are solid rock, worn by the footsteps of the others who came this way before. You cannot see the steps, but you know how it feels to walk down steps carrying a heavy load. You have a choice. You can keep carrying all those weights, or you can carry them down a few steps, and then leave one of the bags on the step you have reached. It is entirely your choice. Do you really need all these negative feelings to continue to weigh you down? Shed them one by one. Keep walking down, keep putting these weights down step by step whenever you feel like it. Keep walking and feel the sack get lighter and lighter and your movement easier as the load diminishes. Keep walking until the sack is empty, and you will then reach the end of the stone steps and find yourself in a beautiful, peaceful, natural landscape. Don't try to see with your eyes – see it with your mind, your memory. It is a place of natural beauty, a place of total peace, and it is a beautiful day. It may take you time to experience this, but give it time. It will come into focus for you. Take all the time you need. You can find a place to rest now, and use the empty sack as a rug to lie on. Stay here for as long as you want, face up to the sky and watching the small, white clouds. Become aware of sunlight gently warming you, and easing your mind and your body as you allow your mind to drift for a while. You can close your eyes and sleep here, safe in this place. And when you are ready to leave, you find that the sky within has already gone dark. It is night, and in the light of a Waning Moon you find your stairway is now lit by the bags on the steps which have transformed into magical Chinese lanterns. As you move onto each step with a lantern, it rises up into the sky. These now carry your hopes and dreams up into the sky, where the Moon can see them clearly and respond. You continue to walk up the steps, and notice that as you look behind you, each of the lanterns which you have passed is now gone. On turning back you see your way ahead is lit. Return to the top of the stairs.

Now you have finished, you can rest for a moment and think about this experience. Then, as before, open your special book, take your pen and start writing. Write down any feelings or thoughts from this experience. Take time over this. There may be more things you want to write down than you would have expected. Don't censor yourself, just write everything that comes into your mind. You can now rest, and will sleep deeply and well tonight.

From now on you will free yourself to use your thoughts and feelings as gifts to others, forming lights for your path when it gets dark, not burdens to weigh you down. When I did this for myself one of the most fascinating effects was that I found other people started to offer me their help – unprompted. Not only was I open to taking their help, but I accepted it in the spirit in which it was given. Once you *give* freely, others will give to you, and the transaction is one of love and sharing, not greed and envy. I recognised that by being able to give to others without the expectation of something in return from them, I freed myself up to receive from those who were willing and able to help me. Each one of us needs others to help us to thrive, and when you are a newborn you need help most of all. That is what the journey into yourself is about. Freeing yourself to be newly created, reborn into this world. It is okay to feel as if you are not yet ready for this. As you read on, so you will change and start to find the best ways for you to move forward.

And know too that the newborn is hungry, not only for food, but for warmth and knowledge. Allow those around you who are able to give you what you need unconditionally to nurture your needs. Perhaps you do not feel that those around you right now are able or willing to nurture you. No matter for the moment. As you travel they will either change with you, or you will leave them behind and you will find others to nurture you. Remember, this is *your* journey, and if someone close to you now is committed to a different path, there will reach a time when you will part. Accept it. It will happen naturally, but perhaps not without pain — for pain is a part of birth. Not necessarily physical, but the pain of becoming someone different makes the new life all the more precious.

Around this time in my journey I started to use the power of the World Wide Web. We truly live in interesting times when we are free to connect with others in such an open and democratic way. Those countries who do not understand the power of the individual yet will regret it — or be forced to change. Newsflash — the time of the worship of money is coming to an end. I know we have all heard this before, but this time it is different. It is global, as are the connections that will drive this change forward. The time of pyramids and hierarchies dividing us is breaking down even as I write these words. The web of lies spun by those in power is unravelling. This is the time for people to take control of their own power, and create, and become part of the True Wyrd Web. Why do you think the old pictures of witches had cobwebs within them? Even then mothers knew the power of the Web. Mother Shipton will teach you how to connect through it, first with yourself, and then with the others around you to weave a web of your own making. To find your community. To seek out those whom you want as part of your life. To put yourself in the path of opportunity.

If you want to change career and become a gardener, you need to learn, and to meet other gardeners. If you want to become part of a spiritual community, seek them out on the Web. If you are finding it difficult to get pregnant, go on to the online forums and talk to others who understand. Create a Facebook page for your street or your community. Get together with a few friends and indulge in a little 'flash kindness' to someone you know needs help but wouldn't ask for it – maybe clean the house of a new mother and cook her lunch or weed the garden of an elderly neighbour. There are more ways to connect than I have time to tell you. So get informed, and then decide where and when you want to get involved. Where your light leads you. It is all about learning. You don't have to rush into it just now. It will happen naturally as you travel on this journey. It will be a process of trial and error too. I went to so many workshops, talks, discussion groups and meetings before I realised that the only way to find the community I wanted around me was to create it from scratch. You may find this too. For me personally I wanted a community of women who are successful and spiritual, who create wealth, abundance and community as part of everything they do. A group who will *share* – share information, experience, knowledge, support. They are not defined by a manifesto or a philosophy; they are led from the light within – the Source. The beauty of this community is that within it we can all thrive. There is no hierarchy, and membership is fluid; there are times when we need closer connection and others when we need to withdraw. It is as natural as the tide that flows within us. Our connection is with Sister Moon, and from within the Source each part of this fluid community is able to become the best that we can be. You will find your spiritual home, your community, your space, but only if you seek it out. You are no longer alone unless you choose to be.

The newborn takes in all knowledge and information, and only filters it later when they have enough experience. For now, all I ask you to do is to read my words, and be like the newborn, open to everything and to remember Mother's words: *Every day you are born anew*. Mother taught me that you have a choice each morning before you are fully awake, as you lie there with your eyes closed. You are free to decide on the nature of your day. You can listen to the rain outside and decide that you are going to have a miserable and dull day, or you can listen to the rain outside and decide that you are going to be the one who makes the day bright. It is that simple. It takes practice to actually *believe* that you are doing it. I *love* that time in the morning, the time before the day and its version of reality comes into my thoughts. This is the DreamTime in which we learn how to experience true connection. This is the time when I have allowed the light outside to awaken the light within me. Failing to make this connection weakens me, and I feel the difference immediately. In this state of hypnopompia I am truly free to create who I am going to be that day. There is no, *I must* or *I want*, there is only *I will* . . . I will be cheerful, I will take control of events, I will be strong, I will find the perfect book for my needs, I will have a good day. Through your experiences in the DreamTime you will mould the day into the one you wish to have. This is the true meaning and power of the sixth sense.

The Sixth Sense

The sixth sense is the sum of the parts of the other five – and greater than the whole. When you allow your five senses to mesh together and work simultaneously – harmoniously – with one another, instead of sequentially – one after the other – your intuition kicks in and your sixth sense will detect those things around you which could be harmful and allow you to sense those which will move you closer to the Source. Start to cultivate this sixth sense – this fusion of the five. Tune into the world around you as you walk and you will start to feel the power of the Source in your surroundings, and begin to feel a resonance within you. You are starting to get excited. You are starting to believe. Cultivate silence. There is an apposite ancient Chinese proverb that speaks of the wise man and the fool. The only difference, it says, is that the wise man speaks little, so those around him pay attention to every word he utters, and the fool talks all the time, displaying his idiocy to the world. It is time to be like the wise man: talk less and listen and observe more. When you do this, you will find that people will pay you attention, even when others are speaking. If you talk all the time, they don't need to wonder what you are thinking and they can ignore you, assuming you are insecure and needy (which is most often the case with people who talk too much). Mother taught me to be still, and sit in the shadows just as her mother taught her. We both learned to listen, to observe and attend to the moods of others. This skill is invaluable. Learn the power of silence. Try it out when you are next in a group of friends. Pay attention to how they sit or stand, how they interact with others in the group, listen to the tones in their voices. You will soon be able to understand their feelings more clearly, like a mind-reader. You will know their needs. At this moment in time, as a newborn, it is only of curiosity value, something to practise, but when you are on your journey to the Source you will find it of real value. You will be able to read the needs of others, and make them your own – if you wish. Mother teaches you this early as the lesson is important, as is the knowledge that you must only use it to benefit others and never yourself. You will learn how to recognise the needs of others and in doing so be able to help them. A word of warning – if you use this power to manipulate and to confuse, you move away from the Moon into the Sun and you will burn up in his fierce gaze. Besides, there are those out there who live amongst the numbers who are far, far more skilled in using this power for harm and they are utterly ruthless too. Never go there – even if you think you are trying to help someone. Never, never, ever.

By speaking less and listening to yourself more, you start to trust the person you are about to become. Through this you will start to hear the voice of magic within you, and you will become free and connect directly with its Source. At first the connection will be in fleeting moments of random synchronicity. At first when you notice it, it will be already gone. The awareness of the Source is not something that you can consciously process. It is a movement seen fleetingly from the corner of your eye. Leave it to the older parts of your brain and you will be able to hold on to your connection when it happens. I will teach you this through trance, and Mother will guide you in the ways to shed your darkness for ever. In the time between waking and sleeping, when you lie awake but are already separated from the world, your mind will open up to the ways of releasing your demons. Start to listen to the Mother within you. She will show you the way when you are completely ready to listen. Don't try to force it. **Open your mind and let it come on each Waning Moon, when you can open your book and choose another shadow-self to shed. You will complete the process on the Waning Moon by burning the sheet of paper on which you laid out your darkness. Name it, action it, burn it.** You will become inventive. Sometimes it will seem that there is no direct action you can take to free yourself. Perhaps your pain stems from a relationship with someone who is now dead. But you can still free yourself. You can write to them – you can clear the air. You can free yourself.

What to do with the sheets of paper, when you have freed yourself by action? By rite, it is time to close the circle with a ritual. This time, with fire.

Mother writes:

At the time of the waning moon
I have named my shadow-self, and in naming I bind it.
It can do me no harm, for I have chosen life.
I release the shadow into the fire
It consumes my pain, and drives all darkness from me.

Closure Ritual

In the evening of a Waning Moon, when the time is right for you, light your candle and open the circle. Take out the sheet which contains your shadow-self, burn it. Have your bowl ready to receive the ashes, and let it burn until there is nothing left but dust. Take the ashes out to the earth. Dig down and bury it if you need to. Mother Earth will take care of the rest.

Repeat Mother's words written above to ensure the darkness does not find space to come back to you.

When I had finished with all my shadow-selves and all pages had been burned away, I mixed the ashes together and buried them in my garden. I planted a rosemary bush in that spot in the flesh of Mother Earth by the light of Sister Moon. I was no longer alone. With them and through them there would be new growth. Rosemary for remembrance, but only to ensure that I remembered *never* to go to those places in my mind again. My connection to the Source was growing stronger each day. As I changed myself, so my world was changing around me, and I was now ready and open to responding to each opportunity to change with it.

CHAPTER **8**

Strength – Dark Moon

—

Trance

Mother writes:

The numbers come to make their play
Hearn leaps through flame and make the players pay
The green man leads, his fee to earn
Pay him well and you will learn
That paper money only burns
Tis time to make the numbers turn.

Commencement Rite

The desire for money as a goal leads to an endless wave of discontent, as there is never enough and yet people think they need more and more to be strong – to be safe. For you it is time to take control of your finances and understand the numbers, instead of ignoring them and hoping they will sort themselves out. Taking time to simply list outgoings and incomings, and to see the need for a balance will help you to recognise that some of your spending has been to feed your emotions, whilst other spending needs to be re-evaluated. Money is a form of power, and it is time to harness it so it can work for you, not you for it. It is time to get practical and create a monthly spreadsheet of your costs and to reign in the energy of your finances to be able to start to control it. You must do this, because if you do not, any money you start to generate will flow straight out again. By knowing your income and outgoings you create a money bowl, one into which riches will flow, and you will be safe to control the power of money. If you need help, seek it. This rite of passage is not an option. With it you gather strength, and start to truly understand that everything around you, including money, is a form of power. Control it or it will control you. I know. I have been there.

To harness the power of money, work at the time of the Dark Moon. The Dark Moon gives no light. No clue. You can stare into the darkness and the only thing you will see reflected is yourself. The darkness causes some to go mad, as can the desire for money. Some fall into the dark light and cannot accept what they find there. You are different because of this journey. You will confront your relationship with money with the rite of passage. It is only in confronting the darkness that you will find the strength to make the journey all the way to the Source.

When I started on this journey, I believed that I had no strength, and that money was hard to get. I had a poverty mind, and this was reflected in the world I experienced around me. I was resentful of others who had more money and who seemed happier because of it. So when I had money, instead of nurturing it and allowing it to grow, I let it drain through my fingers, because that is what I believed would happen. I misused the power of the money I had, and allowed it to be a barrier between myself and others.

Any money I had left over was drained away by those around me. This was the life I had chosen to live. There was never enough money. It was a constant theme in my head. What I was not prepared to do, nor did I understand the necessity for, was to take control. My Dark Moon fell one night in Deptford in my early twenties.

I had just travelled back from a visit to my parents in

Yorkshire to the flat I shared with my boyfriend and another couple. I arrived late in the evening, hungry and cold. It was pouring with rain and, placing my key in the lock I found it didn't fit. There was a new lock on the door, and the lights were off. I had no idea what had happened. So I walked away, back to the Tube station. I sat on a bench and waited. Watched train after train go by until the last train came and went. It must be some sort of mistake – I went back to the flat but nothing had changed. I spent the night walking. I walked away from Deptford and down to Greenwich. I climbed into the park, and my footsteps found the Greenwich Meridian, and I walked along it up to the observatory. It had stopped raining, and the sky was now clear. I continued to walk away until I found a bench to sit on. I have never forgotten how cold that night was, beautiful and cruel and cold. I slept under a clear and empty sky with the dome of the observatory before me, framed in the darkest of moons. My mind emptied as I slept fitfully, crying silently. I was afraid. Afraid of the dark, afraid of what the morning would bring, afraid of the situation I was in. The noises in the park ebbed and flowed as dogs barked, and other shapes took possession of benches close by. No one bothered me. Each form was shrouded in its own darkness.

I watched the morning come with a bleak and watery sun and with it the park keepers. Knocker-uppers for the down and outs. I tried to leave my bench before they reached me, but my body was stiff and cold, and I couldn't stand up properly. A pathetic sob escaped from me, and suddenly I found a hot, dry hand in mine. It belonged to the shape from the next bench along, transformed now into a frail child-woman, more elf than human. I smiled at the thought then tried to pull away, but the owner of the hand seemed surprisingly strong. 'I'm Jennifer,' a voice said in a broad Scottish accent. 'Fancy a wee brew?' Jennifer picked up my bag, and gave me no choice but to hobble after her.

All the shapes of the night, now taking human form, were

heading in the same direction – out of the park and across the road to the back door of a church. Inside it smelled of cabbage and old paper, but it was warm. Smiling women were handing out mugs of tea, and Jennifer was the first in the queue. 'C'mon – if you're quick you get a doughnut. I got you one too.' Hands full she kicked two plastic chairs away from a heap, and sat down smiling broadly. I sat, gratefully taking the tea from her hands. I declined the doughnut. 'You have it.' She shrugged and rested it daintily on her knee. I watched her eat and drink. She couldn't have been more than fifteen – probably less. She ate as unselfconsciously as a young child, but her eyes were ancient. 'See me ...' she spoke jerkily. 'I'm looking for my brother. He came down from Inverness to work, and I'm going to live with him.' She looked up hungrily. 'I'm sure I'll find him today. You got any money?' I shook my head. She brushed the remnants of the doughnut from her jeans and stood suddenly, staring behind me.

I turned to look and saw a tall, skinny man leaning in the doorway. 'Your brother?' Jennifer grinned, showing the gaps in her teeth. 'Aw, hen! My boyfriend.' She leaned over and kissed the top of my head before walking to the doorway, silently palming the flat packet which her boyfriend had passed to her. He kept his eyes on me the whole time. I had seen him before – in the stairwell of the flats where I lived.

It's strange now, looking back on that time. It is all so clear in my mind. I walked home to find my landlady there. I stood on the doorstep to hear how she hadn't been paid the rent for three months and that was it. No rent, no home. I tried to tell her that I had given the rent to my boyfriend to give to her, but she closed the door. No home, no money, no possessions, no boyfriend.

I could have cried, I could have screamed, but I knew that I was not going to spend another night out there on the streets. It was time to take control. By the end of that day I had a home and a job, and was surrounded by men. Wonderful, wonderful men. I traced my steps back to my old home through the market traders setting up their stalls, and past them onto the main road. I took stock and began walking. The sign called to me.

The sign in question was a tatty paper on the door of a club in Deptford High Street. 'Live-in barman required', it said. I pulled the sign off the door, walked in and told the owners that they wanted me. I had my new home. The fact that it was a gay bar and the owners wanted a cute male to attract the customers did not register on my consciousness. I needed them, and I made sure that they needed me pretty soon. I worked and worked, and I loved my new family. I made myself a promise then. I never handed my money – my power – to anyone ever again, male or female. I took control of my money. I didn't yet know how to use its power, or to make it grow, but I had taken the first step alone.

I did go looking for Jennifer. The truth is that I wasn't sure what I would do if I did find her. All I knew is that I wanted to reach out and protect her – somehow. I went to the church, and the women there told me that she had stopped coming soon after. One hinted that she had gone on the game – that the so-called boyfriend had picked off young girls from the church before. I had no way of knowing. What I did learn that night and have never forgotten is how close we each are to the bottom of the pile. It taught me to stop being judgemental when I see homeless people. It taught me to see the people, not their circumstances.

You see, the trouble with modern life is that it contains within it so much noise, so many distractions, too many things to do and to see and to want to possess. All of these distractions pull you away from the Source. Through these distractions I grew weak in the world, and thought that by throwing myself ever more into them I would find happiness, or peace, or whatever I *thought* I needed that day. It was all too easy. To stand still and look inside, and confront the darkness within me – no thanks. That would have meant taking a tour of my own emotional history and having to take responsibility for causing pain, or at best failing to relieve the pain of others. I knew that I had been selfish. Not selfish in a positive, proactive way, but selfish in a grabbing and mean way. I craved like an addict. I wanted possessions and adulation and attention. This is not to say that I got it, but somewhere in a dark and unacknowledged corner of me was a mean spirit – and that mean spirit was me. Until I confronted her fully, and came to terms with her actions, I could not move forward. She would be the dog at my heels like the fool in the tarot. She would pull me back.

It took a crisis for me – a crossroads reached – to make the decision to accept my dark side and come to terms with her needs before I was prepared to call on Mother. I feared growing older and odder and ever more lonely as the person inside me and the one who existed in the world grew ever further apart. I became hard in my relationships with others, and if they displayed the slightest sign of weakness or vulnerability, I would find a way to use it – or at least to store it for possible future use. I was learning from a master, and had no idea of the damage I was doing to myself and to others at this time. When you yourself are brittle and damaged, there will be those who seek you out, and find you to use for themselves. I was empty after the breakdown of my marriage, and, as nature abhors a vacuum, so I was found by a magician – a manipulator of hearts and minds.

He saw a gap in me which could be filled. I understand now that this was not about me – I was not special to him – but part of his manipulation was to make me feel special. He used many people, and discarded the husk when he had no further use for them, or when they grew beyond his reach. He was not a bad man, he was playing out his own story with little care or understanding of the impact he had on others. There are many people out there like that. These are the people who will feed your emotions just enough for you to want to stay around. You become like the starving man, grateful for the smallest pieces of comfort. I no longer fear the man but I did for a very long time. The sound of his voice was enough to cause me physical pain as if my chest was being crushed, and I lacked the oxygen to cry out. Fear is an incredibly powerful emotion, and I feared his power over me, and had no idea how to free myself. I did not understand that I had handed my power over to him and that I had a choice. The revelation came to me when I reached such a low point I felt there was no escape apart from leaving this life. I had never felt that way before, and it genuinely terrified me. I loved life, or at least I had until I fell under his influence. I no longer recognised myself or my actions. I had become one of those people whom until then I had hated – mean, selfish and hard. My heart was full of ice and there was no one coming through the wardrobe to rescue me.

This was the time when I called on Mother. I remembered how she had rescued me before, and now more than ever Mother's words of magic, freedom and life resonated with me. They resonated so strongly that I was prepared to surrender everything I had worked for until that time. I was prepared to undergo death, but a death from which I could return as a new person. The mean spirit within me had to be addressed. It was time to take responsibility for my actions, to release myself from the spell of those who would use my skills for their benefit alone, and to become strong.

Mother's words were clear. On the night of the Dark Moon, when no light reflects on her, I was to communicate with the power of the Crone. The Crone is the aged soul, older than time, older than thought. She is the personification of the Wise Woman – the witch of literature and mythology. She knows *everything*. She is the part of you from which nothing is hidden, nothing can be excused, everything exposed, all laid out to the darkness. I was afraid, and I wanted to set out all my excuses, all my reasons for doing things the way I had. When you expose yourself to the Dark Moon, to the Crone, you do not get that chance. When you expose your mean spirit to the Crone she gives you one choice, and that is the choice to change. No more excuses, just the chance to leave your mean spirit there with her.

When you make that choice, the tasks on your journey become more real, more obvious to you. For me it was to forgive the man I had blamed for the worst of my own actions, and to give back to those who had experienced my mean spirit. I knew that the only way to do this honestly and without feeding the darkness was to give back without them knowing. This way there could be no way of them seeking and thanking me, of feeding my ego. This way was much harder, because all the while the voice of my mean spirit wanted payback and wanted praise. This way I could move forward without all that baggage.

So I took myself into trance. I lay on the bed in the light of the Dark Moon and went looking for the mean spirit within me. I found her hiding under the bed in my grandparents' house. She was small and afraid, and didn't want to come out from under the bed. I was shocked. I thought that she would be big and tough and frightening, but she wasn't. She was only a child with child-like needs to be loved and cared for. I climbed under the bed with her, among the dust bunnies and the books which she had taken there to protect her and to help her escape. She wore boys' clothes, and her hair was short and curly. Her eyes stared into mine, angrily. So I waited, and when she was ready to listen, I talked to her, and told her that we were going on a journey. She knew already, and said that she wasn't going, no thank you. She wasn't going to die. So that was it. That's what she thought it meant, to go on the journey was to lose herself. I lay there beside her, and explained that we were going on the journey together, and that her part of the journey was to go somewhere where she could be cared for, by someone much older, someone who understood her needs and would look after her.

We slid out from under the bed, and I helped her to her feet. She had brought her books out with her, and held them defensively to her chest. We travelled to meet the Crone. Under a Dark Moon, in a rocky landscape, we came upon her cave. She met us at the entrance, and the child eagerly pulled on my hand as she dragged me towards the cave. The Crone was cloaked and hooded. I could not see her face, but I could feel her eyes on me. There were answers in those eyes, but I was not ready to ask. I did not yet know the question. The child pulled away from me, and the Crone's cloak opened to her. For a moment I caught a glimpse of many faces, small and silent, and then the cloak was closed to me. The Crone did not speak to me, but walked back up the rocky slope and was enveloped within the darkness of the cave. I was left alone, with the discarded books at my feet.

Strength for the journey begins with the decision to change, truly change. From this decision comes the emotional power to drive you forward even when you don't want to go, when you just want to fall back onto the old path because it was easier and you knew your way. Strength comes from the understanding that past is past, and you can only change the future by recognising the gifts which you have in the present. Strength will come more easily as you make these changes and magic starts to happen around you. True strength will come when you develop the flexibility and ability to embrace all changes and to see them as a challenge, a test of your worth to embrace the Source.

To grow truly strong you need to recognise the need for support to make initial changes. You need someone to go to for guidance, someone to give you encouragement, and someone who will lead the way and let you lean on them when you need to. This is a person who does not yet exist in the outer reality, but is within you, and comes out of the Source. They will lead you on your inner path to the Source, but they will also guide you to books and people, to places and experiences which you would not have considered as being useful or helpful to you in your journey.

This person is your guide. Your guide will teach you to say

yes to new ideas, and you will meet them in the trance you are about to experience. You may have met them before. They may take the form of someone you know, love and respect. For some they take the form of old, wise beings – ancestors, or even animal spirits. To others they appear as angels. For each one of us these guides are our connection with the Source while you make the journey, and you will learn to accept their existence in your life and to respect their wisdom. For some people, their experience of the guide is of a presence behind them, or a feeling of warmth. You will experience the feeling of someone who is stronger and wiser and is full of unconditional love. You will experience this presence as you open yourself to the Source. Your guide is there for you, and all their guidance is for your benefit alone. You may already know this on some level, but not yet be ready to accept their guidance. It will always be your choice whether you listen or not, and sometimes you will not feel like listening. Your guide will tell you the *right* thing to do, not the easy thing, the thing which we often would rather do instead.

So now it is time for you to meet your guide. As before, read through the instructions first, and then follow them when you have time and space to be undisturbed. Doing this in bed just before you go to sleep is a good time. You will already be relaxed, and your mind is preparing for the inner journey of sleep.

Just before going to sleep tonight, enter your trance by counting down from 300 to zero, using your out breath to time each number as you count down. You will find this gets easier each time. This time, when you reach zero, you can find yourself at the top of the stone steps once again. The steps are solid rock, worn by the footsteps of the others who came this way before. This time you will walk down the steps without any burden to carry, and you can notice how much easier it is now. Notice your surroundings and be aware that the steps are now clearly lit. You feel safer once you notice this.

Keep walking until you reach the end of the steps and find yourself back in the beautiful, peaceful, natural landscape which you have already visited. Feel the peace of this place surrounding you as you look around, and become aware of more of the landscape this time. You may notice flowered meadows and fields of golden corn swaying gently in the breeze. You become aware of rolling hills in the distance, with snow-peaked mountains surrounding them. You are going to head towards the hills, and make your way through the mountains and way up to the highest peak. As you start to walk, you are surprised to find that you travel much more easily than you could have imagined. You also notice that you do not feel the cold, even when you walk up the hills and into the mountains. You can rest whenever you want to, and notice how your view changes as you climb higher. On reaching the peak you can look back and become aware of the place where you rested on your sack the first time you came here. Sit now and rest, here on the peak of the mountain looking down on the landscape of your mind. You can now ask your guide to come to you. Use your inner voice to tell them that you are ready for them to be a part of your life. Now wait. They will come. Soon you will be aware of them behind you, aware of a warm, loving feeling radiating towards you.

You may decide to turn and look to see them, but there is no need. It will be entirely up to you. Your guide now knows that you are ready to make them part of your life. Spend some time in the presence of your guide and thank them for coming to you.

Now leave your guide in the mountains. Retrace your steps back down into the valley, stopping whenever you need. Return to the stairs, and as you walk up the stairs you can still be aware of the existence of your guide as a pinpoint of light up in the mountain. When you return to the top of the stairs you can open your eyes.

Rest a moment and think about this experience.

Once more take up your special book, take your special pen and start writing. Write down any feelings or thoughts from this experience. Write down any questions which you would like to ask your guide when you encounter them again. Take time over this. There may be more things that you want to write down than you would have expected. Don't censor yourself, just write everything that comes into your mind.

Mother writes:

> Strength she is formless
> In numbers when tempered, for there me you may find
> My shape 'gainst the background
> Of gaps in your mind
> Your guide ever truthful
> E'en you try to hide.

Closure Rite

Give away one thing which is precious to you, and you know the recipient will really value, one thing which you would much rather have for yourself. This may be your time given to a task you would rather not do, tickets to an event that you would like to have attended, spending time with an elderly relative, or a present sent to someone you will never meet. It has to be something you value, or it has no worth for the journey. Give it secretly if you possibly can, so that there is no way of your desire for gratitude coming back to you and feeding your mean spirit.

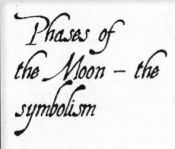

Phases of the Moon — the symbolism

Waxing Moon

There are four phases of the moon which have major significance in connecting to the Source. The second phase which comes after the Dark Moon is that of the Waxing Moon, seen here on the right of the picture. The Waxing Moon is full of potential, and a time to attract what you need into your life. It is a time for growth and newness represented by the Maiden figure, one of the three female figures representing the Moon along with the Mother and the Crone. The maiden personifies newness and purity, strength of intention and courage.

This is a phase of preparation, physical, mental and spiritual. It is a time to gather strength and resources together – to make yourself ready for the future.

CHAPTER 9

Boundaries – Waxing Moon

Ritual

Mother writes:

Prisoner thou art, tho' the gate yawns wide
Prisoner thou will remain til thine enemy within is
    without
Surrounded yet by light you find Aquarius
Pull the arrows from your heart and wake the Draco
    within.

Commencement Ritual

Open the circle. Light your candle and focus your attention on the flame. Let your mind move inwards and away from your surroundings. Spend a few minutes letting your thoughts drift around. When you have done this, write the names of those whom you feel have done you an injustice onto sheets of paper. One name per page. Take your time over this, and if you wish to write down exactly what you feel the injustice was, then do that too. Put the pages into your book. Blow out the candle. Close the circle and put your tools away.

Ivan Illich wrote in *Tools for Conviviality*, 'In a consumer society there are two kinds of slaves: the prisoners of addiction and the prisoners of envy.' When you recognise this to be true then you have a choice about your prison, and whether you want to be free. I know it sounds strange – surely every prisoner wants freedom, don't they? The truth is that there are people who prefer to believe that their drive to earn money is a requirement – something which they *need* to do. There are some things that we actually need to do – breathe, eat, stay warm – but in the last thirty years or so we seem to have forgotten that the desire for a larger car, a better home, more possessions is not a need. Talk to anyone who has been ill for a long time. Simple pleasures become much more significant. Communing with nature. Good friends. Time to learn new things and experience the wonders of this earth. These cannot be bought with money. It is so easy to fall into the prison of addiction to your lifestyle and even easier to envy others around you theirs. It is a trap – stop just for one moment on your journey. Notice around you who are the happiest people. I can tell you from my own experience that they are not the richest – not by any means. The happiest people are those who have stepped outside the prison of consumerism, walked away from the TV screen where they used to watch other people having lives, and started living themselves. Don't wait until your body breaks down with ill health to learn this lesson – *the prison is all in your mind.* You have the key to freedom if you are brave enough to take it and use it. Your fear is natural, and I would be amazed if you did not have some feelings of anxiety at the thought of making these changes in your own mind – but, trust me, I know the difference that freeing yourself from the prisons of addiction and envy mean to your sense of self, and your ability to live life to the full. When you step outside the prison you release yourself from fear.

When I stepped out of my personal prison I was aware of feeling exposed and vulnerable. Our prisons can seem more like sanctuaries – warm and comfortable, safe and familiar. Once you step outside you need to be strong enough to face the dislike of others – and sometimes their hate. They will hate you for no apparent reason. As you travel on the journey to the Source you will find that there are some who seem deliberately set on making your journey hard and unpleasant. Some people who seem to take an instant dislike to you, or hate you before they even meet you. And it hurts. Of course it does. Let me tell you something: it hurts because you allow them into your head. It hurts because you think that it is about *you,* and that maybe, somewhere along the line, you must have done something to offend them and that because of this by your actions you can change their attitudes towards you. Lesson one: *it is not about you.* Lesson two: there is nothing, and I do mean absolutely *nothing* you can do to change their minds. We are all creatures of (mostly mindless) habit, and because of this we will make decisions about people and situations based on how we feel about ourselves at that time. Sadly, this means that sometimes life will seem unfair, and people seem cruel. I experienced this over and over again. So much so that when I came to this part of Mother's words, I found it hard to accept that I couldn't *make* people be nicer towards me. I suppose that in some dark corner of me I wanted to be able to punish those people who were unpleasant to me, or somehow to show these people that their actions and reactions towards me were wrong – to force them to change their minds and to like me. To overcome this I had to recognise a universal truth – you cannot make someone change their mind. But what I did learn is that by being true and honest, and consistent in your actions, you give such people a choice. They can either persist in holding their negative opinions of you, way beyond the time when it is no longer reasonable, or they can change their own minds.

The most precious piece of this knowledge is that by being

true and honest to yourself, you force others to think about being true and honest to themselves, and if they make the choice not to, that is their choice, and you can feel sorry for their loss. Their loss of joy, their loss of the experiences which they could have shared with you, their loss of emotional peace. Sadly, these are often people who are close to you, and are people you want to share in your joy of success and in your happiness. You want them to share it. They cannot or will not because they are locked in their own prison. A prison of their beliefs which they want you to share — a prison which will not allow you to be more successful than they are — even though they are not prepared to put in the effort to be successful themselves. By being successful you are holding up a mirror to their failure to change, so do not expect them to like you for it — quite the reverse will often happen.

I have learned that those who hate without reason often have sad and dark histories, and they should be pitied. I say again — you cannot change them by your interaction with them, but you may help them to change by being true and honest to yourself. They do not hate *you* as such, but they hate what you represent. It may be success, or popularity, it may be something as simple as how you look, or the way you behave. They hate you because you reflect something within themselves, something they are neither willing nor able to come to terms with. I can own this, as I have been there myself, hating people for their success *because I felt that I deserved it more than them.* I was locked in the prison of competition. It was a competition I had no way of winning as it was their game, their resources, their life, their success that I wanted. I didn't realise that I had to find my own and not crave that of others. This way only leads to the lunacy of the Dark Moon. Use the releasing power of a Waning Moon instead to let go of this destructive competition and so prevent these negatives from ever coming back. This is the key to preventing others' hate from hurting you or harming those you care for. You need to create a boundary.

Letting go of negativity helps to create a healthy boundary. A boundary can be psychological or physical, but the essential factor is that it is a flexible and strong boundary, and one which moves with you wherever you go. Otherwise it ceases to be a boundary, but becomes the walls of a prison. A healthy boundary will help you to maintain the strength to move forward, not restrict your movements. If you create a barrier around you at times of fear it will be too small for you, and it will diminish your life by restricting your movements, but if you create a barrier at a time of strength, you are able to let go of your fear and move forward freely, naturally increasing and decreasing your boundaries to let in new people and experiences, and drawing back your energies appropriately when need arises.

Remember your new ritual of waking to the light? Now it is time to know that those precious moments spent in the natural hypnopompic trance between waking and sleeping are the times where you create the space for a mental and emotional boundary. Tomorrow when you wake to the light, you can become aware of the natural boundary of your mind – the space which exists between the inner and the outer you. If you face the world within a prison wall – fearful, defensive and afraid – then it is time for that prison wall to crumble. Tell yourself that you are ready to be free, and have a right to be happy. Watch the walls crumble away. This may happen in one day, or it may take a few days, but when it is gone you are open and exposed to new influences within and around you. As soon as you are aware of this, then it is time to create a true boundary, one which will not only protect you, but will allow you to gain perspective – no matter what the situation. It is not only a boundary, but a filter between the inner and outer realities. Your boundary consists of pure light. Without thinking about it, a colour will come to your mind and you can surround yourself with this colour. Some people feel the colour, like a warmth. Others experience it almost as a sound. For some, the awareness is of the qualities of the colour itself, such as healing, or peace. There are some people who believe they can see these colours as auras around you, and that these colours change. I don't know about that. I've never seen this phenomenon myself, but I do know that my own experience takes the form of a warmth which I feel coming from people. You will find that each day when you wake to the light, the colour that surrounds you will reflect the role which you want the boundary to fulfil *today* so you will always be fully prepared for the events of the day. Remember, the inner reality is what matters most. When you recognise this, then you can, and you will, start to project that reality onto the world around you. You will make your own magic happen. You will mould the world around you and your dreams from now on.

And it is only now when I have a boundary which I strengthen daily that I can say this to you, dear Doctor, who hurt me so with your vitriolic email when my TV series came out: I have allowed myself to forgive you. I forgive your venom and your misguided assumptions about me and what I was doing because I realised your jealousy and ignorance of me and the true nature of my work was eating you alive. I forgive you and hope you free yourself from this pain. I know now that there was no point in writing back to you to explain where you were wrong, and how much you had hurt me with your bile, but I am safe in my protected sphere. I know who I am, and you do not. Yet. And, to you who hurt me so when I gave you so much time, money, energy, and you still wanted more. You who mocked my efforts by calling me 'your pension', and telling me that no one would ever listen to my voice because I am a woman: I forgive you. I forgive you for existing within what I now know was your fear of poverty and your terror of old age. This is your prison – not mine. Do not fear me. I have kept your secrets and I always will. I could go on listing the people, the fears, the memories. And so it will be for you, gentle reader of this book, for when you start to put down the essence of your feelings into your special book you will feel the same. There will always be those who wish you ill, especially as you succeed in your life. It is now time to put them safely in their place where they can no longer do you harm.

The people who hurt you will be those you remember vividly if their effect is still causing you pain, even if and especially when you do not want to remember them. These are the people for whom you have scratched a line on the prison wall of your heart, marking another day, another injustice against you. It is time to free yourself from the prison of *their* pain, and allow them to hate you if they wish. They can hate, but from now on it will no longer cause you emotional pain, for it will no longer penetrate through your protective shield. The space which you are creating between waking and sleeping, the DreamTime, will become increasingly real and strong to you. Its existence will take shape and form and this will be your shield from the emotional harm which others try to inflict on you. If physical pain is part of your life story, this is the time when you make sure that no one will ever be able to hurt you in that way again – because you are taking control as you grow in respect for yourself. You can and will remove yourself from negative spirals of influence, whether this for you is a person, a drug, a situation. I know this may seem difficult or even impossible for some of you right now, but your journey to the Source is also a journey away from fear and pain. *You are no longer alone* unless you choose to be, and the boundary you are about to create will give you the security, the strength to start to make some of the bigger decisions. Let go of the pain, let go of the desire to please those who would do you harm. Release the hurt into the shade of the Waning Moon. Let Sister Moon draw out the poison, and leave you free from pain and ready to heal.

Closure Ritual

Light your candle once more. Focus on the light there, and feel the warmth of the flame. Allow yourself a few moments to connect with the warmth of the flame and let it kindle and echo within your breast. A flame burns there too. Close your eyes for a moment and continue to see the echo of the flame imprinted on your mind's eye. Take time to register the light within you responding and feel the warmth of both Sources of light – the light without you and the light within.

When you have finished, take the pages on which you wrote the names of those who hurt you without cause, and tear them up as small as you can. Tiny, tiny pieces, as small as you possibly can. Extinguish the candle flame. Now water must take the pieces. Go to a stream or river, and drop the torn pieces into it. If you do not have a river close by, the toilet will do. Flush those fragments away. Let Aquarius carry the pain from you.

You can use the words below to end your closure ritual.

Mother writes:

The portal opens its maw to me
I will fear no longer
The indivisible surrounds me with love
I give my gifts in secret
And seed the flowers that grow on my path.

CHAPTER 10

Healing – Full Moon

||||

Rite

Mother writes

In healing t'other tis balm to oneself.
The dart in thine breast twas shot from within
Self love begins when self harm ends
Thou must love me to own myself.

Commencement Rite

Having allowed water to carry away the fragments of dislike, hate and fear, the next rite of passage is to ensure that you do not accidentally wander back to this same prison in future. The most direct thing, and often the most difficult, is to learn how to send out positive emotion to those people. Not neutral, not to ignore them or to try to cut them out of your life, but to give to them the emotions which you would have them give to you. **Before you can do this, in the mornings when you wake to the light and become aware of your natural boundary surrounding you, take time to strengthen that boundary for the day ahead.** You can do this by pouring more colour into the mix, or even changing the colour to something which you feel will be of more value to you. Start to trust your feelings and do not *try* too hard at this stage. What you need will start to come to you. The time of the morning light and the space between waking and sleeping will start to have even greater significance to you as it creates the direct link between the magic of your inner world and what you will choose to project outward during the day.

I have to be completely honest with you at this point. I personally found this rite very, very hard to do. I cannot pinpoint whether it is my ingrained English cynicism or my scientific rationalism that reared its ugly head at this point, but I found myself in donkey mode. You know what I mean – the donkey that doesn't want to go somewhere, and just sits down and *nothing* can move it. I just couldn't imagine how this was going to enhance the magic in my life. Okay, I had to admit that all the stages which I had been through on my journey up to this point had brought rewards – sometimes direct and sometimes oblique, but there was always a clear benefit, a step forward. I now recognised that my life *had* started to change, and the goals which I had set myself were starting to take shape in the world of my outer reality. I had started to ask for help, and receive it. I was really starting to believe in the version of reality which existed in my mind, one in which I was successful and happy, free and fulfilled. Events and coincidences which I could only call supernatural were now becoming commonplace for me. The changes were all starting to happen, and I was beginning – just beginning, mind you – to trust in the process. But this? What possible value could there be in sending out positive thoughts and feelings to those who had hurt me? Surely it would be better for me to preserve my good emotions for those who deserved them – and what about me? What about self-love? I didn't buy into it at all.

So I ignored this step. Well, what would it matter, really? I was getting on really well, and the fact that I couldn't see its value meant that it wasn't relevant to me. That's what I chose to believe, anyway. So I carried on doing what I had been doing up to this point, paying close attention to the early-morning rite of waking to the light and strengthening my boundaries. I was doing fine. Then, suddenly, it all started to go wrong. The production company making the television series was taken over by a large American conglomerate, and I went from walking my path to a headlong slide down. I was about to learn why the word 'career' has two meanings. The name of the series was changed from *Hypnoconfessional* to *Sex, Lies and Hypnosis,* and I was no longer in control of events. I *hated* what was happening. Now I had a genuine concern that my oh-so-modern wish to be famous was about to backfire – horribly. I didn't get much sleep during that time, and could feel my boundaries shrinking away from me like the gums of an old crone. Why had that image come to me so strongly? I could feel the shade of Mother Shipton moving my rocking chair back and forth, and it started to get on my nerves. I had a choice. Get back on the path and move forward, or let all the magic slip through my fingers like so much sand.

So I did as I was told. I listed all those hateful people on individual pages, I wrote down all the events and the feelings, and when I was done I tore those sheets into the smallest of pieces, and walked to the Thames. My river. Okay, so it is also the river of millions of others, but I know it as part of me. Part of the magic. I walked to the middle of Westminster Bridge, and waited for the wind to change so it would carry my torn-up pages into the grey artery of London. I let the pages go, and watched them flutter down to the river. Gone. Now the hard part, to send out positive emotions and to take positive action for those people whose hate had got into my head. Don't get me wrong: I was still feeling resentful. I felt as if I was being forced to do something that was against nature, against myself, but I did it.

It was so hard for me because the hurt was much older than I chose to acknowledge.

When it first happened – and it didn't go on for long, not like with some people – I was eleven years old. I got book tokens for my birthday. I was growing up. There were three of them, but really it was only one boy and two watchers. They were a year older than me. I knew them from school and could avoid them there. It was on the walk home that I was vulnerable and they picked me off like parka-clad crows. Some say that no child is evil, but in the heart of the ringleader blackness was condensed into his diminutive frame. Adulthood did not dilute it, but gave him less scope to inflict pain. I saw him not so long ago. There was no recognition in his eyes when he saw me watching him.

This was also the first time I actually remember being visited by Mother, but let me put this into some order so you can see clearly. When it happened first, I was scared and confused. I felt that I was ugly and alone. I had no idea what was happening to me, just that it was a secret and that if I told anyone about it I would die. This much I believed, I *knew*. For five nights afterwards I stayed awake as long as I could, and from my window I watched Mother looking for me. I could feel her seeking me out. She looked in the other houses in the surrounding streets. I could see her moving around the bedrooms, and peering out of the windows into the night gardens. Her dark looks frightened me more than what was happening, and I tried to learn how to fly away before she found me. When the night finally came when she appeared in my room, peering over the bed to look at my face, she sniffed like the witch in the gingerbread house story. I thought she had come to eat me, and I didn't mind. Not too much, anyway. That way I would be safe, and it wouldn't happen again. I raised myself up on my elbows to look at her properly, and she smiled. A wide, toothless smile that weirdly made her look like a very young girl. I smiled back and she raised her gnarly finger to my lips to prevent me from speaking. She taught me how to fly. To fly away so that when it happened again I wasn't there. At first, I could only fly downwards, and in a sort of spiral motion at that. The first time I did it I found myself back downstairs, watching my parents preparing for bed. I watched my father walk out of the room and switch off the light as he left, regardless of the fact that his wife still sat in there, reading. I watched her stillness as she sat in the dark, alone. By my foot, Mother pulled me roughly back up into my room. *That's not what it's for, child. You mustn't use it to pry. It will only end in tears. Yours.* I dropped my bottom lip sulkily, but soon recovered when Mother flew me out of the window. *This is what it is for!* I could feel her hand holding me, and the sensation of the air around me, but I couldn't feel cold. I watched snowflakes settle on her cloak as we flew. I was free here. We went out to the Peaks, past Old Man's Head, and landed in a heathery field. The sheep turned to stare at us, as Mother guided me to a black rock where she signalled me to sit. The sheep followed. *How come they can see us?* I asked. *They see me, child. You are not here.* I didn't ask more questions. There was no reason to. She had come for me, and taken me away. Mother had taught me how to fly. For that I was grateful – unquestioning.

I could fly to her on my own from then on, and would meet her by the farm in Agatha's cottage and rest my head on her lap while she told me stories. I found sanctuary by her hearthstone. She told me lots of stories then. Stories about magic. Stories about numbers. Stories about people. She poured the knowledge into my empty head, and sealed it away to be released in its own time so it, too, wouldn't harm the child that I was then. She held my head in her rough hands and made me promise that I would keep the knowledge safe until others were ready for it. Until the day when I was ready to open the door in my mind. Until I was the teacher. I promised, and yawned wider and wider until, lulled by the heat of the fire in the hearth, I slept. I could feel her hand stroking my hair and hear her gentle crooning.

I did try to tell others. I did try. Somehow the words

wouldn't come. The threat of death was real. I didn't want to die. I wanted to survive – to live. So I bit down on the words, and my skin went blue and yellow and green from the effort. I sucked in hard to stop the words from leaking out of my mouth, and watched the blood seep up through my pores. I became a chameleon in the hope that they wouldn't be able to find me any more. I bit down on my pain.

My mother saw it, and cried. She thought it was about her – that there was something she had done or not done. She wouldn't believe that I was doing this damage to myself even when the doctor moved my limbs around marionette-like to show her how I had done this to myself. The doctor matched the marks to my lips. Mark to lips, mark to lips, a parody of painful kisses. I saw pain in my mother's eyes, and I stopped biting, but decided to never speak of my own pain. I knew that the words would burn my lips so I kept them within me. Burning. I was a survivor.

The last time it happened and my mind took flight to Agatha's cottage, there was no fire in the hearth, and Mother stood in the doorway, dressed for travelling. She took my hand even though I didn't want her to. I knew then that she was taking me back there, to them. To be there as it happened. I closed my eyes tightly and waited in stillness for it to begin, then I saw Mother smiling at me and I felt her step into my body. I was to be a marionette once more, but this time the scary kind. She used my voice, and the acid from the words coated my speech with corrosive power. She used my limbs to lash out and fight. I opened my eyes and saw them recoil as they fell into the black eyes of mothers. Many, many mothers. Their own. Their fathers' mothers, their own mother's mothers. Her eyes in my head looked at their faces and told them their greatest fear – that they would die alone and in pain. The words came from inside their heads and rooted them to the spot. I closed my eyes and fell as Mother left my body. Breaking the spell, they ran from me. From us. My eyes teared blood in payment for her act. She left my body empty and returned me to safety. I don't remember going home, or going to bed, but I know she stayed with me as I slept fitfully that night. Each time I woke she was there. Sitting in the corner of the room. Muttering musically under her breath. Always the same phrase. Just below hearing, but somewhere deep inside me I responded. She was there. Ever vigilant. I was safe. It wouldn't happen again. It didn't happen again, and she weaved her words and sealed the doors of that history as well as she could. She locked the door and preserved my sanity with its bolts. The memory was imprisoned and left to rot until there was nothing left but dust. It was enough for me. I could survive. The chameleon in me stayed on, though. Not the blue and purple skin, but the invisibility I learned then. I could disappear if I wanted to. I still can. I survived.

But to heal myself through pity for those who had done these things to me, or even through love? That to me felt like a different story. Mother's instructions for this part of the journey came at too high a price. She asked me to send love out to those who had harmed me. I couldn't do it. I made a choice. Pity? Mercy? Maybe. Love, no. Some of those people were now dead to me, either physically dead or so far removed from where I was now that there was little I could do to reach them anyway. I bargained with myself on this part of the journey – and you may too. It is about choice. I chose a partial healing. I could hear the words of John Lennon's 'Crippled Inside' as I decided on this route, and knew its true meaning. There was not enough strength in me, or willingness, to send out love to those who had harmed me so deeply. I bargained that to keep a little of the pain was a price I would choose rather than give love to those who had hurt me with malice and deliberation. I chose pity as my balm.

It was the hardest act of all for me, to send out pity to those people each morning when I woke to the light, but I now know that with this act I healed myself. It wasn't about them any more, their thoughts or feelings – it was about me. So to those people I sent out pity with a capital P. Unconditional Pity. A Pity that could or would not be returned and expected no reply. A Pity that in some dark part of me I knew would cripple them if they could know about it because it meant I had taken back my power. A Pity which for those perhaps who had been hurt in their own time would bring some peace.

I made a decision to reserve love for those who enriched and nourished me. I would not and could not love those people who had done those bad things, but it was time to give them my Pity. If this was to make my journey to the Source harder, then it was my choice. Just as each step you take and how far you choose to go with it is your choice. It all became about choice, just as it will for you. The things you choose to do, those you choose not to do, will determine the speed which you travel and the path you take on the way to connect with the Source.

I doled out my Pity person by person, day by day, even when I did not have names for those people. I did this during the time when I connected with the light each morning. I strengthened and thanked my boundary first, and then sent out Pity to each and every one of those people. Each day it got easier. Each day the corrosive resentment lessened. Each day I noticed that I moved closer to the path, and instead of a headlong slide who knows where, I was back in control again. I had taken the career and shaped its meaning to conform with my inner reality once more. I had the magic back.

The others, those with whom I had different stories and were still present in my life, required more than just the sending out of thoughts. These people required action. This was the price that I had chosen to pay to progress on the journey to the Source. My arrogance in deciding what I did and did not need from this process was teaching me a simple lesson. All of us, in some shape or form, need to pass through each stage of the journey. Some will be easier than others, but it is not for you to deselect any which seem difficult. You have to earn your connection with the Source. I earned mine through words as well as deeds. At first, I wrote letters, thinking that I could create an easier option than making direct contact with people who had hurt me. Then I realised that this would not be enough, and the letters, as well as telling those people how they had hurt me, went on to tell them that I would welcome them as part of my life – and that I forgave them and asked them to forgive me if there was anything in my behaviour which had prompted their reactions towards me. In writing the letters I could feel those people with me in the room – but the weirdest thing was that I didn't fear them any more. They could not hurt me because I was taking control. They were strange letters to write. Even stranger to receive, I should imagine. Only one from my recent past contacted me, telling me that they did not want to hear my excuses and telling me never to contact them again. I found that especially interesting as at no point had I attempted to excuse my own behaviour. The words I had written to them had changed form when they hit the prison walls of their own mind. For me, I had fulfilled my part of the bargain. I had given freely and with as much love as I was capable of giving to each.

Once I had completed these letters, I knew that I was back on track. I could move forward, and by strengthening my boundary every day I would never put myself in the prison of someone else's negative emotions again. Each day when I sent out positive feelings to those people I could feel the gaps in my boundaries healing. I was growing stronger through these actions. I soon came to realise that in my inner reality I had the right to say no, and to leave others and their problems outside this safe space. I could leave other people's opinions of me in the outer reality and not carry them around as a burden in my inner world. Without the negative emotions of other people invading my inner reality things became *so* clear. I now knew that I had a right to care for myself first. I would take time daily to value and strengthen my boundary whilst I rested in the light. Most of all I would be prepared for any others who would try to climb into my head and manipulate my magic. I was back in control.

Mother writes:

No more the Fool, lest love is lost
To love the other comes at no small cost
In loving Self comes selfless pace
Know Maiden, Mother and Crone all will earn their
   place.

Closure Ritual

Open the circle, light the candle and focus on the light from the flame and reflect on the power of the morning light, and how you feel when you connect with it. Open your book and write down your thoughts and feelings. Close the book and hold it in your hands. Close your eyes and feel your way into the words. Feel the power of the words which you have already written there. From now on, make time in the evening to write down any events or coincidences from the day which you feel are signs that you are on your way to the Source.

Tomorrow, go online and register as a PostPal. With this you agree to write to, support or send gifts and cards to a sick child. With this act you offer hope and love to those who will most benefit from it, and you will get this love back, manifold. Supporting a sick child stops you from feeling sorry for yourself, and reminds you what is really important in life. People. Good people. Become one of them with this act.

Imbolc

Traditionally this festival marks the first day of spring. It begins at the start of February in the northern hemisphere, and at the start of August in the southern. Imbolc was merged with St Valentine's Day, and is a fire festival designed to draw the warmth back into your life and home.

This festival is dedicated to the Maiden phase of the Moon, and is regarded as a good time to work on healing the body, discovering activities and actions which will improve your physical wellbeing.

Because Imbolc is a fire festival, it is customary to pay attention to bringing natural light into the home, freshening the rooms with natural sunlight and using this to see what changes need to occur in the home.

It is a time to notice the feelings which come with the return of the light, and use these to create a sense of renewal at this time. As part of this it is customary to rededicate your home, and spring-clean.

Rituals associated with Imbolc include making promises or pledges for the coming year. Imbolc is a time of starting projects and being inspired by the world around you as it awakens. It is a time to light candles and illuminate the dark places in yourself preparing for reappraisal and change.

A time to welcome the new.

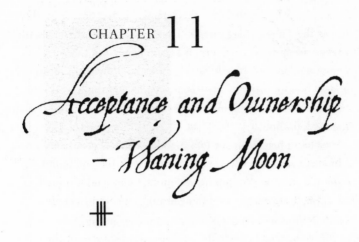

CHAPTER 11

Acceptance and Ownership
– Waning Moon

╫

Trance

Mother writes:

Give to those who ask of you
Take from those who give
Give and take will make you learn,
Own your journey as then will all gifts return.

Commencement

Do you own your time and space? Or do you allow the needs of other people to flood in where there should be barriers? Get out your special book and, on a new page, write down the names of all the people who you believe *need* you. Once again, do not censor it; this is an exercise to bring your beliefs out onto paper so that you can put them into order. When I talk about need I mean those people who come to you first for help. If you have children or are responsible for adults who physically or mentally cannot fend for themselves, their names do not belong on this list as their need is legitimate. The people I am talking about are the *needy* ones. I am sorry if I seem harsh, but these are the emotional leeches, people who take without giving in return – and at this moment in time you are *allowing* them to do this because it feeds a need in you. Write down the names and close the book for now.

When I had given out Pity to those who had given me pain, I found myself in a strange place. I felt emptier without all the hate and history clogging up my mental space, and there was an emptiness within me. I did not realise how dangerous this space is. Mother had not given me enough warning of the perils of this time, which is why I feel the need to warn you.

Without all the hate and the history, you are in danger of falling into a trap – and this is the trap of trying to heal others. A good trap, you might think at first, but it is a dangerous place to spend time. Believe me. Having healed myself I felt empowered to pass this healing knowledge on to others. Okay, perhaps 'empowered' is not the right word here. Perhaps 'arrogant' is more accurate. You see, I felt so wonderful, and so strong having let go of the weight of history that I wanted to share this feeling. I knew that I could spot the others – those whom I could help. The others were those whose eyes were hooded and looked inward. Eyes like I used to have. I heard them in the countryside talking to their dogs. I saw them commuting in the packed London Underground. I felt them next to me in the darkness of the theatre. So many others – and all with the same eyes. Eyes that had seen too much. Eyes that projected the same film over and over onto the screen of a private movie theatre. One seat only, and the best in the house for the others. One film – on continuous play. Over and over and over again. I could help them – I knew I could. I wanted to share my freedom.

And herein lay the danger. A very real danger to my progress to the Source of magic. I had very quickly forgotten how far down I had to go before being willing to heal. I had deleted this from my mind and skipped over the work I had to put in, and past it, onto the wonderful results. This was the danger for me. It had completely slipped my mind that one should *never* ever offer a gift, especially one of this magnitude and life-changing power, to someone who hasn't asked for it. You can have no idea where they are on their journey, and most of them will reject your offer, and resent you for trying. You stand outside their experience like an accusing evangelist, offering a new life. Offering freedom. Learn from my mistakes. Some people are not ready to be free. Some people do not believe they are captives of their past. Some people are *happy* as they are. It took me a while to accept it, but there are many people out there who did not want my brand of healing – and if they did not seek it out for themselves they will reject it and mutilate themselves even further with your offer. Walk away. Do not offer help where it is unasked for. If someone asks, then that is a different matter, but don't try to help if no one asks you. You yourself will end up resentful and frustrated. I know. Been there, done that, got the T-shirt and frequently irritated people along the way.

And then there are the others. The ones who come into your life with gifts. Remember that you put it out there that you wanted help, so the help is appropriate and wanted. These are the people who are willing to share their knowledge, their time and their energy with you because they understand the root of their own power. These are not passive people – these are activists. They may already have come into your life and you dismissed them as 'lucky' or 'privileged', and because of this you have chosen not to ask them for help. If they are as secure as they seem, they will not mind you asking; in fact you will find that these are the people who enjoy sharing knowledge. They have accepted and understood that they not only *own* their power – their magic – but they understand that with rights come responsibilities. What I mean is that they understand that we all benefit by sharing knowledge and by building connections

– building a web based on mutual understanding and respect. We all need help to achieve our full potential. This is the time to accept help from others, and to value that help, and – when you are ready – you will be prepared to pass it on to others. You are part of the Web – and passing knowledge and help on forms part of the connections needed for the connections to thrive. Accepting help is part of owning your journey, recognising that from now on no one is going to *make* you think, or feel, or do something which does not feel right for you. Now you are at a stage when you can think about doing this, you can open yourself up to receiving these gifts freely.

I recognised that throughout my life there have been people who have tried to help me. Help with time, money, patience and understanding – so many gifts and at the time I did not accept them in the spirit in which they were given. I either tried to pay them back with other gifts, or I ended up resenting these people – thinking that they were being condescending or that they were feeding their own senses of superiority by helping me out. I do know that this was true for some of them, but for the most part it was me who got it wrong. This happened to me because I feared the relationship in which I believed these gifts placed me – I feared being beholden to someone else – and so I spoiled the gifts even as they were given. It was as if I believed that I did not deserve the benefits of the gifts which people were trying to give me, so I deliberately screwed things up. I did not *want* these gifts to help me because I lived with the mistaken belief that if I didn't create the success all on my own it had no worth, or that somehow if I thrived by allowing others to help me they would own my success and I would always be 'less' than they were. I couldn't move away from comparing myself and my success with other people and what they had achieved. Such a complete recipe for disaster. And so a perfect set of self-fulfilling prophecies came about. I decided that people would not want to help me, and so they didn't. I allowed myself to resent the givers of gifts instead of being thankful. In the end, people stopped trying to help me because it all became so complicated and awkward. I created the situation where I was given no more help – and persuaded myself to believe that was the correct order of things.

It all changed for me only after I asked for Mother's help. When I called on her I had reached rock bottom. There was no one else in my life who would listen to me any more. I had pushed those who had tried to help me as far away as I possibly could, and surrounded myself with people who needed things from me – people who took from me but did not give me anything in exchange. I became the solitary giver. I wanted to be the one sitting at the top of the mountain dispensing gifts to those who needed help. I mistook this for power. Yes, people came to me for help and I felt needed, but Mother's words soon made me recognise that these people were feeding off me, and that instead of growing powerful from their needs I was allowing myself to be drained by them. There was a seductive danger in believing that you were the only person who could help someone with their problems – so seductive that if someone called on me for help I would drop whatever I was doing and go and help them. Of course they were grateful – of course they praised me for my help – but all the while my needs, my dreams, my path shrivelled and grew pale through lack of nurture. For goodness' sake, I didn't even have plants at home any more as I was never there to care for them.

I needed guidance, and Mother gave it to me with her words. I had pushed her aside when I was a child, but this time I came to her as a child would, helpless and crying. We all need guides in our lives, and before we can recognise the physical guides who will come into our lives, we need to identify, connect with, and open a channel of communication to our inner guide.

It is now time for you to bring your guide from your inner world, and make them heard in your outer space.

Just before going to sleep tonight, enter your trance by counting down from 300 to zero, using your out breath to time each number as you count down. When you reach zero, you can find yourself at the top of the stone steps once again. You can start to feel the familiarity of these steps, this place of nature. Walk down the steps until you find yourself back in the beautiful, peaceful, natural landscape.

The fields and the meadows, the hills and the mountains are all there as you remembered them. You can just see the mountaintop in the distance where you met your guide. Return to the mountains and once more meet your guide. This time, ask if they will leave the mountain and come back with you, and to come into your life. Wait for the answer. If the answer is no, ask for permission to revisit them in the mountains in your sleep. If their answer is yes, and they are prepared to come with you now, ask your guide to lead the way back to your life. You can then follow your guide back down the mountain and into the valley. Notice that your guide carries a lamp with them like the hermit in the tarot lighting up your path so you can feel safe.

Return to the stairs, and as you walk up the stairs you are aware of bringing your guide into your daily life. You will start to feel that you are no longer alone.

When you return to the top of the stairs you can open your eyes.

Afterwards, you can rest a moment and think about this experience.

If, for any reason, your guide did not come with you this time, don't worry. They will come in your sleep and your dreams, in your DreamTime, and when you need a sign that you are on your way to the Source. You will hear their voice and see their signs. You will feel their presence – it will happen for you when you are fully ready.

Once again open your special book, take your pen and start writing. Write down any feelings or thoughts from this experience. Take time over this. There may be more things that you want to write down than you would have expected. Don't censor yourself; just write everything that comes into your mind. You can now rest, and will sleep deeply and well tonight.

You have invited your guide, you could even say, your higher self, into your life. You will be aware of their voice and their guidance more and more each day. That is not to say that you will want to listen. The likelihood is that you will not be fully prepared for how it feels to have a guiding voice telling you what to do, think and feel. You may (as I did) start to feel that you are being treated like a child, and in response you will start behaving like one. I thought that having a guide in my life would make it easier, and that everything they said would be *nice* and encouraging, that it would mean that they would only tell me things I wanted to hear – you know what I mean. I thought that having a guide would be like having my ego massaged whenever I needed it. Yeah – right! You try having a discussion with a 500-year-old witch – you can't *ever* win. The fact is that the reason you need a guide is because you wandered off course in the first place, so a guide will dictate how and when and what you should be doing. Once again I repeat - you have a choice. You can either listen and find that decisions get simpler, or you can bridle and argue with them, and lose the path again. Your guide carries the light of experience of treading the path to the Source. They know the way – and what is more important is that they know the right way for you. When you feel the presence of your guide, listen and pay attention to what they tell you. In doing so, you will travel light and fast and, most important of all, you will travel in the right direction.

Mother writes:

Learn stillness, and study those around you.
Accept all new information – the time to filter comes
   later.
Allow others to feed and nurture you.
Start to seek out like-minded people
And let the others thrive with your neglect.

Closure Ritual

Open the circle and light your candle. Clear your mind by
taking three deep breaths and allowing your thoughts to flow
towards the centre of the gentle light. Open your special
book at the page where you wrote down the names of your
needy connections. Take your special pen and draw a line
through each one in turn. As you do, silently say to yourself,
*Today I free you to find your own path. I will help you best
now by standing back and letting you help yourself.* When
you have done this, close the book. Close your eyes, and
once more go into the heart of the flame with your thoughts
and slowly bring yourself back to the here and now. Open
your eyes and rest for a while.

   You will soon notice that those around you who took up
your time and energy needlessly and with their neediness *will
change.* By changing your reactions to their requests you will
allow them to grow and develop, something which you were not
allowing them to do when you used to do everything for them.
It is only by standing back and letting others make their own
mistakes that they will grow from child to adult in thoughts,
feelings and actions. Your needy friend may become a true
friend from this. Those who reject your new strength and want
you to continue to serve their needs are not true friends. Cut
them loose. They are on a different journey to you.

CHAPTER 12

Home – (Dark Moon +

Trance

Mother writes:

Home is within you
It inhabits your dreams
Home is without you
Closer than it seems
Home is your saviour, home is your friend
Home is the road for some will never end
Look within, for without you wither
Make no mistake and hurry hither
Dark Moon will show you what you lack,
Harken close, and bring home back.

Commencement Rite

Home. This is the place where you can make your new reality manifest first. You will find what you want in this space. The fire as energy and your sense of balance will come to you here. The focus on home in a Dark Moon may seem an unusual one. After all, the Dark Moon is the Moon of psychic forces, of dreams and desires, but is also representative of absence – of emptiness. Your home should be a place where you feel safe and secure even in the dark, even when you are the only person there. When you find yourself alone in your home, walk around it and allow yourself to become aware of the different feelings which come to you as you go from room to room. If there are any rooms where you feel negative emotions or sensations, make a note of it in your special book. Also note the spaces which make you feel particularly calm or happy. If you get no feelings from your home, make a note of that too. You will work with these emotions (or lack of emotions) at the end of this chapter in the closure ritual.

Lunacy is latent in a Dark Moon – just as you can find erroneous beliefs about home. You probably know someone (or perhaps you are that someone) who has got entangled into a home life which is unhappy, or even in some cases dangerous for them. Most often, if you discuss this with that person you will find that they can explain to you all the reasons why they cannot leave this space. *My children need the security of two parents; My partner has threatened to kill themself if I try to leave; It isn't how it seems; He is always sorry afterwards.* A seemingly endless litany of excuses for staying in this dark and dangerous place. That is the lunacy of the Dark Moon which you need to be able to confront to make a true home.

Home should be a place of love and nurturing, a place where you want to be above all others, a place to come home to and to be safe. If it is not, then it is not home, but simply a place where you live. More accurately it is a place where you exist rather than live, because without these feelings of safety and security it is very difficult – I would say virtually impossible – to become one with the Source of your magical self. Living without security causes everything you try to create to be unstable – vulnerable.

The first thing to recognise is that you *do* have choice. The choice to leave or to stay. When you recognise this, the next choice becomes simpler. If you choose to stay, then it is to work *with* your partner to create a safe and loving home − a place where you can both be honest and caring of each other, and allow each other to grow and develop. It is a hard decision when you feel that you still love someone, but you are changing − you are growing closer to the Source − and they are not. Their journey is not the same as yours, and you may find that the differences become too great to sustain. It is *not* your fault for changing, and if your partner tries to lay guilt on you for this, you can, and you will, let it go as part of this process of homebuilding in the light of the Waning Moon. Remember, this process is not *making* you change, it is bringing your desire to change into sharp focus and giving you access to the tools and the strength within to make the changes for yourself. Once you have a clear understanding of the place which you call home, you can homebuild on solid foundations, either from within that relationship, or from outside.

In the past, I did not know what home meant. I thought (notice *thought* not *felt*), that home was a place with furniture and possessions, and the people were the least important element. I discovered through my journey to the Source that the possessions did not matter *at all*; in fact during this time I was burgled. Things which I believed to be of great value were gone from me for ever, and my feelings about the place in which I lived was changed. I felt it had been tainted by this invasion into my privacy. The truth of the matter was that the next day I woke, and in the most weird way possible I felt liberated. All those *things* which I was fiercely protecting were gone, and I was still alive. Instead of feeling diminished, I felt free. And the feeling of vulnerability left the house when my friends brought love and sympathy to me. The concern they brought overwrote the feelings of violation, and I started to realise that it was only the people who mattered. That's all. Simple as that. People who cared and brought their love for me hidden in flowers and food. I started to learn the real meaning of home.

Further back, in what feels like a past life to me now, I

was in a relationship with a man who also did not know what home was. He brought the only ideas he had about home, and recreated them in the place where we lived together. This was a time in my life of noise and alcohol and rich food, of parties and a constant stream of people. A time too of voices raised above the music in public argument. He made the noise happen because he feared peace, hated silence. Above all he feared death and oblivion, and his way was to fill the home with vitality. There was no corner of peace in the home, and my mind screamed out for rest, but the screams went unheeded, muted by the constant beat of music and laughter. We parted. I wish him happiness. I wish him some corner of home where he now has peace. I can truly wish him love now, but it was a longer journey to those thoughts than I would have hoped. Mother hadn't yet come back to my thoughts at that time and I felt completely alone. At that time I was made deaf and blind by my partner's sadnesses and fell deep into the lunatic deception of the Dark Moon.

I felt spiteful and mean. I would clean obsessively after the parties, some of which I wasn't even part of as I had started to work away from home just to get some peace. Things started to disappear from the house and he had no idea how it could have happened. I felt that I had no home. If any of this resonates with you, do not fall into the trap of blaming the other person for this. They built the only home they understand, *and you brought your home with you too*. Sometimes the template is wrong, that's all. It may be one of you, or both of you. Either way, this is why, as a therapist, when I treat people who come to me with recurrent relationship problems I ask them why it is they think that they repeat certain 'mistakes', such as seemingly always finding an alcoholic or abusive partner. The answer is simple – *unconsciously you seek them out*. It is like the pieces of a jigsaw puzzle – you fit together because you already understand how to behave in these weirdly dysfunctional circumstances, and in the end you start to believe that this way of life, this pattern is inevitable. It is *not*. You can use the Dark Moon to allow yourself to register the only things that matter to you in a home. In the Dark Moon you can see clearly what is missing from your home. What does it lack? Does it lack a heart, does it lack security? In the void of a Dark Moon you can allow yourself to imagine the previously unthinkable. What if you lost it all tomorrow? What would you mourn? It is the strangest sensation.

Many, many moons ago, I walked out of the place which I then called home. I took my graduation clock, a couple of photographs, a family teddy and a few clothes. What did I miss? Nothing. Objects can be replaced. I quickly forgot about those things which I had filled my space with. I was no longer defined by the things I owned. Ironically as I didn't learn the lesson fully at the time, I was doomed to repeat it until I got the message, so I filled my new habitation with more possessions, only to lose them all over again. Ask anyone who has had a house fire, or some devastating force of nature wipe out their home, and they will all tell you a similar story. Mementos. That is all they would save. They rescue the irreplaceable, not the valuable in the more usual sense – that of financial value – but memories. A home is a place to create and to store memories. Nothing more. When you have experienced the absence of home in the Dark Moon then you know that home is a space which you carry within you. It is not a physical space in the obvious sense, but a mental space. Home becomes a place which you can take with you wherever you go. Home for me, now, is time with my husband, access to books and my friends, and space to write. I can be at home anywhere. Home is what you create for yourself – it is the inner peacefulness created from knowing that you would rather be here than anywhere else at this moment in time.

When you confront home in the Dark Moon all the areas missing from your home are highlighted. If peace is absent, or time for each other, or love – that is what you register, and if you cannot shape your current home into one which gives you what you need to feel safe, then it is time to change. Discovering lack in your home life does not necessarily mean that you need to leave that place. In fact this can often be the worst thing to contemplate because it may lead you straight into another home which is just the same. You see, because you carry your image of home with you in your head, you take it with you to the next place, and the next, so *you* are responsible for the home you live in. No one has forced you into this space, and no one can help you out of it other than yourself. Remember, you are on a journey. You can't expect to reach the destination immediately, and sometimes you need to remember where you are now so you can make sure you move in the right direction. Now it is time to become one with the journey again.

Remember to enter trance in your own way in these sections. You can imagine taking part in this scene, or, just before going to sleep tonight, you can enter your trance by counting down from 300 to zero, using your out breath to time each number as you count down. As before, when you reach zero, you can find yourself at the top of the stone steps. You walk with more confidence this time, as you feel more familiar with the landscape each time you visit. Notice your surroundings and be aware that the stairs are now brightly lit, and you feel safer now you have noticed this.

Keep walking until you reach the bottom of the steps and find yourself back in the beautiful, peaceful, natural landscape which you have already visited. Feel the peace of this place surrounding you as you look around, and become aware of more details in the landscape this time. There are flowered meadows and fields of yellow corn swaying gently in the breeze. Notice the sounds of nature around you.

You notice the sound of a river. Go towards it. There are reeds and grasses by the river. There are also trees. Allow yourself to be drawn to one particular tree. It is an ancient *Duir* – an oak tree, with a solid trunk, and you notice the deep, gnarled roots burrowing into the earth at your feet. Look up. Notice the branches and the leaves. This tree is strong. You can lie down now beneath the tree, and close your eyes. The oak is a doorway to deeper knowledge.

Rest beneath the oak and notice your breathing. Notice the sound of the leaves in the branches as though the tree itself were breathing. You find that your breathing starts to synchronise with the tree itself and you connect to it as a living entity. The tree invites you to share its essence — to know what it is to have ancient natural knowledge and be connected to the earth. You find yourself starting to drift away, allowing the tree to take you on a journey through root and branch.

First the tree takes you deep, deep into its roots. You feel the connection with the earth.

Now the tree takes you through its trunk, and you experience its strength.

Next you journey all the way up through the branches and into the topmost leaf and you feel movement as the leaf is blown around in the wind. You allow the wind to move you as you feel safe. The tree is sharing with you three qualities: connection, strength and flexibility.

Move away from the oak, and travel back through the landscape. Return to the stairs, and as you walk up the stairs you can still feel connected to the oak and the qualities which it has shared with you. You will hold on to these feelings and they will be there for you whenever you need them.

When you return to the top of the stairs you can open your eyes.

When you have finished, you can rest a moment and think about this experience. If you wish to write in your special book, do so. Otherwise, read on.

Mother writes:

Clear and cleanse and banish
Your home needs heart and mind,
Shed light on hearth, no shades of past in nooks and
   crannies dwell,
Home is here when love is near, it's heaven now not
   hell.

Closure Ritual

Create an ancestor corner. An ancestor corner can be likened to
a hearth. Whereas a hearth is a focal point for heat and a place
where people gather, an ancestor corner creates a gathering
point for positive energy.

This is a place where you put photographs and mementos
of people who are or have been close to you and who you feel
have shown you love. Do not put photographs of anyone here
who does not fit into this category. When you have this in your
living space you are connecting yourself with those who make
your sense of home a real one.

When you have created your ancestor corner, light a candle
(preferably one in a glass container so you can carry it safely),
and ask each person represented in this space to give a little
love to the candle flame. Then carry the candle all around your
home, into every space you went to before. Illuminate all the
dark corners with this candle light. With this you are claiming
the space around you with the love others give to you. You are
making this space a home to be filled with love.

You can make use of the ancestor corner at different times,
as and when you need to. For example, the anniversary of a
death or when you want to be particularly close to someone
from this group who is not in close physical proximity to you at
this time. You can light a candle before their photograph and

close your eyes. Call them to your thoughts. Spend as long as you need with them. Ask for their love and support. Talk to them. When you have done so, blow out the candle.

By doing this you will fill your living space with strong loving energy which will protect you. The way you feel about your home will change. When you have lived and communicated with your ancestor corner and are comfortable to have it in your home, go back to the book and open it on the page where you wrote down your feelings about the place you live. Either you or the space itself will soon be ready for the changes you need to have a real home.

Phases of the Moon – the symbolism

Full Moon

The Full Moon, with her maidenly aspect, comes next in sequence after the Waxing Moon. This is the Moon of the Mother – a time when things which you have put into motion in the Waxing Moon will come to bear fruit. It is a time of the greatest psychic energy, strength and ability. It hangs fat and full like a pregnant belly. Magic spells cast in the light of the Full Moon are powerful change spells. The Moon is at its height of magical influence here, and if you work with this phase, expect the results to happen soon.

It is considered good to work with groups in the Full Moon, especially for spells of binding or healing. You can also 'charge' objects with the magical energies of the Full Moon by leaving them out in the moonlight and letting these objects 'absorb' the lunar magic. Water, crystals and food are traditionally left out at Full Moon, and the water and food is taken when the practitioner needs the energy. The crystals can then be worn for magic work or as an amulet for protection when feeling vulnerable.

The Full Moon is also a good time to go out yourself and absorb some of that otherworldy light. The ritual called Drawing down the Moon takes place during this phase. To draw down the Moon, go out into the full moonlight, and stand with your arms raised, palms upwards.

Traditionally this is a Goddess ceremony and therefore performed exclusively by women, but there are no hard and fast rules. Anyone who wants to fill themselves with the power of the Full Moon and to invoke the help of the lunar Mother aspect can perform this ritual.

Personally I approve of a little moonbathing, especially for the stressed. It calms the angry mind and facilitates physical healing. I find that it helps to focus your attention outside yourself, and so improves your perspective on events. It stops me taking myself and my needs too seriously, and allows me to remember how small I am in the cosmic scheme of things. Not a bad thing if your ego has a tendency to swell occasionally.

CHAPTER 13

You are not your past – Waxing Moon

T

Ritual

Mother writes:

Sever the Gordian Knot
Not tease at the threads
Birth your Dreamtime to breathe the air around you
Do it now and watch the Chaos fly.

Commencement Ritual

Start to allow yourself to pay attention to those moments between waking and sleeping. The moments at night when you have gone to bed, but you are not yet fully asleep. Notice how warm and lethargic your body feels, and make yourself aware of what you are thinking. Just observe. These are the moments when you are in bed, waiting for sleep to come to you. This is the time when you are most aware of the recent past – the day which you have just had.

For now, just be aware of this transient state. What you need to do in this state will come with the closure ritual at the end of the chapter.

Until I called on Mother Shipton my past was like a roundabout. I seemed to keep coming back time and time again to certain beliefs about myself and the world, behaviours and even types of relationship. Events seemed to repeat themselves. Different people, different places, same outcomes, same old me. There seemed to be a certain inevitability about how my life would play out in future, as if it was already mapped out for me. It was as if my past was my future. I found that even if I started on what seemed like a new path, the habits of the past kept coming back to me, and I was stuck in the old groove again. Out of frustration I tried many different ways of escaping from the patterns, but inevitably I failed. You cannot escape from yourself, and it was me who created the patterns even though I did not want to know it at the time.

When I finally reached the stage where I was prepared to accept Mother's advice, I truly felt that there was no hope of change for me, that I was who I was, and that I couldn't change. After all, aren't we all products of our upbringing and experience? Mother taught me that it may be true, but it is not all there is. Most of what I thought to be intrinsically part of me, deep-rooted character traits that I believed to be fixed and unchangeable, she taught me were simply habits. Patterns which I followed, but they were not actually *me*.

She reminded me of the original meaning of the word 'habit'. A habit was simply a garment, a piece of clothing. It was something you could put on or take off *when you needed it*. You are *not* your behaviours, just as your habits can be put on or taken off when you need them. As soon as you realise this, once again you have choice. I no longer behaved with the old knee-jerk reaction to events, and allowed myself time to *decide* how I was going to react. This was hard at first, of course it was, but once I learned the trick of using the night Web which I will show you in the closure ritual at the end of this chapter, I found it much easier to do. It is a form of mind training: just as, many years ago, you trained your mind in the habits which harmed you, so it is time now to consciously train yourself into the habits that heal. This does not happen immediately. It takes around three weeks, about twenty-one nights before the training kicks in and you 'forget' that you are doing anything different. The effort wears off as each day goes by, and your new ways of reacting become your natural default.

Now I want to turn your attention to the relevance of this in connecting with the Source. This is mostly about your relationship with the past. The past for you may have been the most wonderful time. It also may have been awful. For most of us the past is a mixture of both, and how we react to the past also depends on how we feel right now. In terms of our memory, the brain connects with similarities, you see. So if you are feeling down, your mind associates with memories of feeling down. If you are feeling upbeat, these are the connections which are reinforced – the mental patterns which are activated by mood. Your past is a state of mind, not an absolute reality. It is your perception of history, not an accurate record of the events that happened. For some people it is more real to them than their present, because they are reliving events from the past over and over. When you do this there is little or no room in your inner reality for your future. I mean for you to understand that not everything you believe about your past is a fact – an unchangeable event. Your past is a moveable feast, one which changes each day as your perception about yourself and the life which you are living changes. You adapt your ideas and feelings of the past to fit what is happening to you right now. We will often forget our actions of the past, especially if they do not reflect us in a good light. We can also forget the actions of others, whether good or bad, depending on how we feel about that person right now. It becomes easy to idealise a good event from our history. It is also just as easy to take an event that was bad and continue to suffer from it. When it comes to our own personal past, we are the authors of the history. This is not to say that we lie to ourselves, or actively *try* to change the past, but it is a part of human nature and human behaviour to need to catalogue our past in order to understand it, and ourselves, better and in doing so we can create a version which fits with our needs now.

The easiest way to get to grips with this thought is to keep in your mind the fact that no matter how good the meal was that you ate last night, remembering what it was like will not nourish you today. The past is there for you to learn from, not to relive or regret – this has little value in your future and only small value in your present. The only real value lies in using the past in helping you to understand how you are the unique designer of the patterns of magic which you allow into your life, and that *nothing is fixed as part of your inner reality* unless you make this happen with your mood states. Good memories collect around good memories, but this only happens if you are in a good state of mind when you enter sleep. Conversely, bad memories collect around bad memories when you go to sleep in a bad mood. You dictate what gets remembered and how – what sticks in your mind. This is why the mood you take into your sleep becomes so important.

Each night when you go to sleep, you enter a different state of consciousness, which changes and develops as your sleep progresses. You take your mood in there with you too, and because of this it will shape the way in which you remember events which have happened to you in that day. In your sleep your mind makes short cuts to memory, based on those emotional states. In your sleep state your mind experiences many different processes, among which is a set of sequences that helps you decide how you will respond to the next twenty-four hours.

In your REM (rapid eye movement) sleep you enter a memory-consolidation and future-preparation phase, helping you put the events of the past day into context, and helping you change your mood to a more positive one as you do. This period also helps you create ideas of how you are going to act and react with the events of tomorrow based on your memories of how you have reacted to similar events. Oftentimes, when we are feeling a little tired or disconnected, this is when we get a feeling of déjà vu in our waking life. This is because your mind has already experienced the events which are about to happen. It has already created them in your sleep and has mentally rehearsed them so well that you feel and think as if it has already happened to you. What is more, you have now already experienced the event. Because your mind has played out the scene in your sleep and your dreams and because you are tired, this projection of events is mentally experienced slightly ahead of the event. You feel as if you know what is about to happen to you.

The incredible part of this is when the event plays out *exactly as you already experienced it*. It astounds me that most people just accept this and feel no need to understand how astounding and life-changing the knowledge is that you can *accurately predict the future – your future!* This to me is a prime example of everyday magic which most of us sweep under the carpet of life and ignore. Not me. When I started to work within Mother's framework I recognised that I could change the world around me using this knowledge. I decided to use this knowledge to plan my future. By creating a positive mood just before I slept, I would decide which memories would become real for me, and how I would then be able to experience the world around me. With this knowledge I could plan and predict my own immediate future. I was pushing the magic beyond myself and my inner world into the outer world of reality. My magic then became something which others could see and hear and feel. The feeling was astounding to me as day after day I experienced my life as a sequence of events *just ahead of them happening*. I was starting to make magic happen, and could feel the Source was starting to work within and around me.

The only way in which I can describe this happening is that it feels a little like pushing my hand into water. I only displaced what was immediately around my hand, and when I pulled away the water returned to fill the space. This is the nature of changing reality – even for a brief moment. You could even call chaos theory's butterfly effect into play. By only allowing the positive feelings into my sleep at night, I was going to create my future emotional template as a positive one. I was going to be able to *plan* my feelings about the future, and each time this happened it would reinforce the ability to plan for happiness and success, regardless of the events.

The fact is that you already prepare your future, even though you are not consciously aware of it. Because of this lack of awareness, you allow the standard background program to run in your head which allows your unconscious mind to shape your future based on your past. It does this because you do not tell it to do anything different. Currently, when you go to sleep at night you replay the events of the previous day. You will not be aware of this consciously; it may be a process of which you are completely unaware. Sometimes you may register it is happening when you start to drift off to sleep and a particularly annoying or upsetting event trips the switch and makes you aware of the thought. Most of the time, though, you allow this program to run without interference. The only problem with this is that by doing so you are letting all the events of the day into your inner world – your inner reality – and thus you are changing it. To make your magical future and connection with the Source a strong reality, you need to start filtering out the thoughts and feelings which are potentially damaging to your future. Not everything needs to get through, and to do this you will create a filter through which only the positive and useful will progress into your inner space.

Once I discovered this knowledge, I decided to make a

conscious effort to plan my next day. I mentally rehearse journeys, conversations, and unexpected encounters, all in the moments between waking and sleeping, and most of them without even me being consciously aware of what I am doing. It has become a habit – as it will with you. Let yourself experiment. I create the mood and the outcome. I focus on the positives that have happened to me during the past twenty-four hours. I then daydream of my next twenty-four hours in an ideal world. Of course I do not always get the outcome I expect, but by planning my part in the events I make sure that I am going to have the best possible experience. Now I no longer rely on my memories to paint the pictures of my future. I allow myself to get excited and I plan for successful encounters. The most wonderful thing about this is that the more it happens, the more new positive memories I collect, and the more likely I am to have positives happen to me. I look forward to my life, and by doing this I take this positive mood and future image of events into my dreams, where I continue to work on them. This way I am never disappointed by events as my dreams allow me to play out my reactions even to disappointment. I create a state which means I will usually be able to find a positive, regardless of the actual outcome. This is both realistic and positive, allowing me to understand myself better and to benefit, regardless of what happens. You will find this both a strange and a wonderful experience. It is like having a secret, which, if you even tried to explain it to anyone else would have them glazing over or running for cover. Magic sometimes needs the cover of secrecy. Keep this to yourself and let others discover it for themselves. They will see the changes in you soon enough.

Closure Ritual

From now on, when you go to bed, take a few moments to imagine a web suspended above your head. You can imagine a spider's web, or a web made of beautiful silver silk threads, or even a traditional mandala – a dream catcher. It is entirely up to you what sort of image works best for you. Allow the image to become as clear as possible in your mind's eye. When you have done this, tell yourself that all the events which happened during the day can now flow into your mind, but only through the filter of the Web first. All of your thoughts will be funnelled through the Web above you. You may notice objects and images clinging to the Web, or the Web itself changing colour in places where thoughts are captured. Only the events of the day which will add to your learning or reinforce a positive state of mind will get through. Don't worry about what gets caught up in the Web, as when you sleep it will be cleansed and repaired, and everything which got caught up there will be swept from your thoughts. Nothing will get through that can harm you from now on. Nothing which will prevent you from reinforcing your connection with the Source will penetrate the Web of Wyrd.

For this is what you are creating – a Web of destiny. From now on as you filter your experience of life and only take on board that which will help you, it will all become much clearer to you. You will understand what to do much more easily. You will know what is good and what is harmful. Wyrd – destiny – is about to become part of your life now you have created the filter. As each day goes by, you become more aware of the positives around you. More aware of the coincidences. More aware of the exciting potential of creating and of stepping towards opportunities. Life is about to get exciting. Look around. It is all starting to fall into place as your inner reality begins to take shape and form around you. It is starting to happen. Allow yourself to feel it.

Use the night Web whenever you have had a particularly challenging day. Otherwise, let it happen when it feels right to you.

CHAPTER 14

Loving – Full Moon

✛

Rite

Mother writes:

O Sister Moon, pregnant and full
Use your silver alchemy to turn my dark side bright
Give me strength to forgive myself and embrace the
    Source
I will share your silver with others in return.

Commencement Ritual

Who are the people around you who make you feel *less* than good about yourself? The people who, when you meet them, leave you feeling angry or depressed, or just not good about yourself. Take out your book and write down their names. There is a reason for you to write the names in your book. It is so that periodically, when you review the contents, you check that there aren't other names who need to be written down and dealt with. This is enough for the moment. Close the book and put it away.

So, now I ask you, when was the last time you took time

out for yourself – whether to do nothing at all, alone, or to treat yourself to something which only you would enjoy? Was it yesterday, last month, last year or never? Do you care for yourself and your needs in the way that you should – the way, perhaps, you are happy to treat others, but not yourself? It is time to start showing yourself the love that you want to get from others. It is the simplest of tasks this time. Each week, schedule time for yourself. Time which is set aside for you, alone. Time which is not negotiable. You schedule in things which you don't much like, such as visits to the dentist or taking the car to be serviced, it is time to give yourself time. I schedule *me* time before all else – and I do not negotiate. I will only change the contents of this time if something I would rather be doing instead comes along – and then the rule for me is that it must be something which is to please me – not to please or appease someone else. Diary. Now. Put in '*me time*'. Do it every week. Consider yourself told.

Yes, I know. I am well aware of what you are thinking. Easy to say and not so easy to do. Do not try to skip this part – it is essential to the journey. Don't think either that you can do it for a little while and then allow the needs of others around you to creep into this time, thinking that it won't matter. It does and it will matter, because if you do not respect yourself, you will not complete the journey. It really is as simple as that. You need to recognise and to feel that you are worth the journey – that you are ready to be magical and one with the Source. To be part of the Source and to stay connected to it you need to start liking and loving who you are. Now. Not when you are thinner or richer or smarter – now. I can tell this to you now as someone who got completely lost and went right to the edge before an angel pulled me back.

One of the most difficult kinds of love is the love of self. Shakespeare knew what he was talking about in *Henry V* when he said, 'Self-love, my liege, is not so vile a sin, as self-neglecting.' Most of us have been brought up to fear self-love and confuse it with selfishness. Loving yourself does not mean that you are being selfish – it means you know your own worth, and you respect yourself, your body, your ideas, your right to occupy your space. It is a fear of appearing arrogant or selfish that drives many people to be their own worst enemy, treating themselves with less respect than they would a complete stranger. Perhaps self-respect would be a more comfortable term than self-love. It still means the same thing. Let me put this to you – do you value your own opinions, and are you able to say no without feeling uncomfortable? If you are, then sadly you are in the minority. This must change if you are to become one with the Source. Those who live in the Source know their own worth and prize their skills and contribution to others. Most people, however, have got into a habit of valuing others more than themselves, and they lose out on life as a result. Their lack of self-respect tells them how others should treat them, and they end up getting no respect from others either. It is time to change – time to embrace your honest and magical self and time to stand up and give yourself some Respect with a capital 'R'.

I admit, it isn't always easy when you are working against a lifetime of conditioning and, as in my case, I had brought myself into close contact with someone who was more than happy to reinforce my lack of self-love. This person was happy to see me confused and sad and used these states to manipulate me. It wasn't personal. I was just one in a line of many. At the time I couldn't see the harm which was happening and I didn't love myself enough to be able to step away from the attention which he paid me. I could not step away from this man even when I heard him tell another, 'You are nothing without me. It's cold outside – remember that.' I didn't think that I was being unfairly treated, and I worked ever harder to try to gain the respect from him which I was failing to give myself. I was like the starving man in a desert as I begged for scraps of attention. Looking back I cannot honestly remember who I was. At that time in my life I was out of my own head and so busy trying to fulfil the needs of others that I had lost sight of who I was. I only knew when I had had enough of this empty life.

Picture the scene: Newcastle in the north east of England. It was winter, just coming up to Christmas. I was working there through the weekend. It was how I spent most of my weekends at that time. I remember that it was a Friday night, and Newcastle comes to life at the weekend. It really knows how to party. The nearby docks were full and as the evening drew in I could hear the sound of men singing and the laughter of women close by. It was only early, but the ships were in and the sailors were out for a proper, good time. I watched the scene from my hotel room. I remember it was a nice hotel, bland but inoffensive. The rooms looked like many others I had stayed in before. I would know my way around this room in the dark, even though I hadn't stayed here before. It was designed that way. Anonymity accented with low-key modernity. It left me feeling well and truly depressed. I expected I could even guess the room-service menu. I looked. I was right. I turned to look outside. The best thing about that room was definitely the view.

My room overlooked the quayside, and the Millennium Bridge spanning the Tyne with real style. The winking bridge, they call it locally. I never did find out why they call it that. It was beautiful, though. Especially as it got darker and the lights on it shone out into the darkness. It started to look more ethereal, less like a bridge and more like a gateway to another place. I looked on. With the darkness came snow and I watched it settle on the roofs of cars in the street below. I leaned on the window, looking out on the scene below, and registered how cold I felt. This was not just the cold of temperature, but the cold of ice veins. The cold of non-existence. The cold of a room made to be inoffensive to all and appeal to none. That's what my life had become. Bland and anonymous. And it was all true. This had become my reality and I had created it, or at least allowed it to be created around me as I lost the will to create my own. I was ceasing to exist as a person. There were no calls asking me out to play on Friday nights, or any nights, for that matter. My obsession with my working life had put paid to any invitations that used to come. People get tired of asking when you always say no. I was becoming ever more numb as I watched life in the street below me. I remember thinking at the time that I couldn't remember exactly when it happened, but I knew then that I had looked out of too many hotel windows at weekends in too many cities. If I didn't exist any more, what was the point of carrying on? Who would miss me, I mean really miss me? How can you miss someone who is never there anyway?

Looking down I saw three women arm-in-arm, singing carols loudly and with energy. I wondered what they would have thought of me had they looked up. I was spending my weekend in solitary confinement watching others having fun. I changed focus and started to see my face reflected in the dark window. A blank expression greeted me. I didn't like what I was seeing, so I retreated into the room. Turning on the TV I flicked aimlessly through the channels. Reality TV heaven. Other people's lives to vicariously enjoy for those like me who had none of their own. What to do now? I could order room-service, or I could just walk out of the hotel right now and throw myself off the Millennium. I remember thinking that it probably wouldn't take long to drown in the cold dark Tyne. I pulled on my boots and wrapped up warm. At least I wouldn't get cold on the way there.

When you make a decision like this, when you are stone-cold sober, (I couldn't comment on the sane part, I can only tell you that I felt sane in those moments; in fact it felt like the sanest, most logical act of my life in that moment of thinking), the oddest things start to happen to you. Your limbs move on autopilot. You feel your heart bouncing around inside as if it is trying to remind you that you are still alive. I can only tell you that the first thing that came to my mind was that, now I had made my mind up, I had just better get on with it. No point in waiting. I left the hotel, crossed the road, and made my way to the centre of the bridge. It was still only early, and there were lots of other people around. I decided to come back later, oddly blushing at the thought of being the centre of attention if someone tried to stop me now. Better to wait. So I walked. I walked through the packed streets aimlessly. What I wanted to know was when this city would go to sleep so that I could get some rest – finally. And so I walked. And walked and, well, you get the picture.

Many tired hours later I found myself close to the top of a tall hill, looking down over the city. In those hours of walking I started to feel more alive than I had in months. Maybe it was the reality of the biting-cold wind and the snow, maybe it was the sheer effort of walking. I couldn't tell you what I was thinking then, but I do remember how it felt, and it felt good. The snow had continued patiently all evening, swirling in corners and piling up, making the hard edges of the buildings soft and marshmallow-like. It had turned the usually drab buildings into Christmas decorations – toys for the festive season.

From a distance I could hear solitary shouts from the city itself, but here, on this uphill street I was alone. Almost. I looked to the top of the hill and saw a young woman. She was not dressed for the weather, wearing the smallest of dresses and the highest of heels. I almost didn't see her, as, with her back to the bus stop, she had slid down until she was sitting elbow deep in the snow. The snow had already settled peacefully on her head and shoulders. I walked up the hill towards her, concerned that she would freeze to death, or maybe already had. I just wanted to make sure she was okay.

As I arrived, she stirred, dislodging her snow hat behind her. She looked up at me calmly. 'Fancy a chip, pet?' From her lap she pulled a soggy chip from a paper bag. 'Keeps you warm, chips does,' she mumbled, then started laughing. I couldn't help it, I laughed too. 'My chariot has arrived.' With this she waved her arm vaguely in the direction of downhill to a bus toiling its way up towards us. I helped her stand and get onto the bus. Only then did I see the tiny nylon wings, complete with damp feathers, strapped onto her naked shoulders.

She waved to me from the back seat of the bus as her 'chariot' carried her home to heaven. I laughed all the way back to my hotel. I laughed until I cried. An angel saved my life that night, pet. An angel in the last place I was looking. I got back to my room and ordered a plate of chips in her honour, still laughing. I knew then that I didn't want to kill myself, but I did want to put an end to my current existence – to the ice maiden which I had become. She was cold and hard and unpleasant in my eyes. She had been trained like a dog to act and react to the world around her – mainly by one man but mostly by her own weakness. I recognised even in my depths that I could not blame another person for who I had become. I had to accept responsibility for myself, and instead of killing her, give her respite. Rest and peace, something which she/I did not have in the life we were living. It is she who sleeps now on that Scottish mountain. I stopped hating her, and learned to understand what had created her. With Mother's intervention I took back control, and for you it is time to learn to love your inner reality, and to give form to your dreams and hopes with others *as if they are already real*. Because, guess what, they already are real, and ready to move outside your inner into your outer reality.

Mother writes:

With original sin you were marked at birth, they say
I say, nay,
Their power wanes as your Moon waxes
You were born to live, not wait for death
Take your first steps
Face the world and learn from Seth.

Closure Ritual

Open the circle once more. Light your candle and meditate for a moment on the flame. Go to the pages on which you had written the names of those who reinforced your negative self-beliefs. Send out healing or feelings of gentleness to them – as much as you can afford.

By doing this simple act you will remove the poison from your heart, and open yourself up to positive experiences. It is time to free yourself to love yourself with all your flaws and imperfections. It is okay. You are work in progress. If you fail to do this you create a block which prevents you from opening your heart fully to love and you will return endlessly to the roundabout of negative emotions and relationships. It is truly time to move on, time to love yourself, warts and all! If you don't, your boundaries will solidify once again into prison walls and you put yourself straight back into your old prison. It isn't easy, but it gets easier. Love is a beautiful and natural drug, one which fuels your inner reality – your magical world – and helps you to push it into the outer reality, linking with others.

Beltane

This festival begins at the start of May in the northern hemisphere, and at the start of November in the southern. Beltane is known in some cultures as Walpurgis night, and celebrates the male and female power.

This festival marks the start of the summer, and the shift from dark to light. Life force is strong at this time of year. It is a time to light fires to protect you from harm and to cast out the echoes and reminders of harm done to you.

It is, most significantly, a time of purification and transition, and is a good time to make decisions about change. The rituals associated with Beltane are ones relating to new projects, love and romance, fertility and creativity, and renewal of commitments.

Fires are also lit at this time to remind us of community and care, and as a way of reminding us about hearth and home and its importance, even though the season is about to move into a time which is more associated with being out of doors. It is therefore a time to remember those who are restricted in some way, either physically, mentally or emotionally, and to encourage them out into nature, where they can respond to the life force of Mother Earth herself.

CHAPTER 15

Thoughts – Waning Moon

||||

Trance

Mother writes:

Paradise was the home to Adam and Eve
But they knew it not
Count your blessings
Lest you lose the Lot.

'Thoughts become things.' We have all heard this or something very similar before, whether from yogis or coaches, but have you ever stopped to think what this actually means? This phrase is too often misinterpreted by those who would rather believe that all they have to do is *think* about something and they can make it happen – they can manifest it externally just by putting the thought out there. These are the people who, sadly, do not put any real effort into their lives, somehow expecting everything to come to them. These are often the people who also misunderstand the true meaning of magic. The true meaning of this phrase is about the power of our own words – our inner dialogue – to affect how we interpret the world and our own place in it. To quote the Stoic philosopher, Epictetus, 'Men are disturbed not by the things that happen, but by their opinion of the things that happen.' This is as true now as when it was said all those centuries ago. This is reality – not the stuck-record version of your life which you currently inhabit. Reality based on perception, not on events. It is based on faith and belief, and honesty – not on power and influence. True magic is personal, and the Source joins us together within the Wyrd Web of connections around us. Like electricity, we do not see it, but we see its effects. And it is through words that we express our true reality.

When the words within are words of *power*, then this will become the basis of how we interpret the world. Mother brought me to understand that if the only words which I gave to myself were words like 'fear', and 'helplessness' then these were the ingredients for the trances which I would live on a daily basis. Make no mistake, I use the term 'trance' deliberately. For if you do not believe that you can do magic, I have an urgent newsflash for you: you have been casting spells of influence on yourself ever since you were able to think.

With the words you choose, you create an image, an internal reality which you then project onto the world around you. You start to live in a daze based on what you expect to see, hear and feel. Everything else you will reject as being outside your version of reality, and therefore act as if it isn't there. Let me give you an example. If the words you give yourself are 'miserable' or 'unlucky', this is the trance you will live, the filter through which you will interpret the world. You believe it to be so, and it becomes so. With these words you are casting a spell of power and darkness onto your inner reality. You may not have consciously chosen these words – no one initially does set out to be negative – but these may be words which were given to you by life experience or from the words and beliefs of others around you, and you *chose* to make them your own. You will therefore feel every ache and pain, and think about what it might mean. You will expect your relationships with other people to be negative, because this will then reinforce your experience of the word 'victim'. Please understand me – I am not saying that your illness or bad experience is not *real*, but to a degree you accept the words, and do not fight the negatives. You start to believe it is something intrinsic to you, and not just words. Words become reality because we give them power to create trances.

I recognised that the words which I had chosen to entrance me were many, and nearly all negative. My words created a spell of failure, and anger, and fear. The trance I lived was one of self-sabotage. At the time you don't even register the words, they are so much a part of your inner vocabulary, your way of communicating with yourself. The first thing to do is to take a step back from your thoughts, and to actually *listen* to what you are saying. The next step is a dialogue between the part of you using these negative words, and the part of you ready for new ones. Then and only then can you open yourself to interpret the world in a new and positive way. Then you will start to see the world around you change in response to this new way of thinking. All you need for a wonderful, magical life is out there already around you in your world, but you need to remove the blinkers, take out your earplugs, and reach out to touch the beauty around you.

I had found that the easiest way to make the connections was in a meditative trance, just as I am guiding you through in this book. I gave myself the time and space to enter the trance between waking and sleeping, where the ability to listen to thoughts, to inner dialogue is at its most strong. As I have taught you, I counted down from 300 to zero, and when I had reached zero, I rested for a while and allowed my mind to wander freely. Just to wander and wonder about things that were happening in my life at that time. I allowed my inner voice to ramble. This time, I started to pay close attention to the words – the phrases – and then the quality of this inner voice. I very quickly noticed an irritating, whining tone. It wasn't loud at first, but the whine grew louder the more closely I listened. The inner voice was complaining. Not big complaints, but it was a theme. I became aware that the phrases my inner voice was using contained things like 'unfair' and 'I bet it won't happen, anyway ...' This inner voice was talking me out of the dreams I believed that I had. My inner thoughts were preparing me for failure *before I had even started*. As I continued to listen to this voice, I began to notice recurrent themes: failure. Why even bother because it won't work? Other people do these things, not you. Keep your head down and nothing bad will happen. If you are too happy then something terrible will happen. Don't look forward to something or you will only be disappointed. Keep your head down and expect little from life. Set phrases. Programs waiting to be run just for me. I was well and truly shocked. No wonder I felt low and dispirited with this audio track of misery running through my head. I took a deep breath and introduced myself to this inner voice. *Hello*, I said. *Can I help you?*

The voice paused momentarily, then continued with the catalogue of complaints. I repeated my words. The voice responded, *Why do you want to help me?* That caused me to pause. This inner self obviously did not believe that I could possibly want to help. *I want to help you, so you can help me*, I said. I could feel the owner of the voice crossing her arms defensively. *Well, that will be a first*, she said. The more I listened to this voice, the less I liked the owner. *You don't even like me – why should you want to help?* she said. I felt sad and dispirited at this. She had a point. I *didn't* like her very much. She was the sort of person I would rather not be around, the sort who, if you phoned her up with some good news would quickly turn the conversation on to how miserable she was and you would end the call feeling depressed.

I sat down next to her, so she didn't have to look at my face. *I want to understand why you are like this, so that I can be free. Be happy*. She stared out into neutral space while I glanced at her profile. Her face was contorted in lines of sadness. Her jaw was clenched and tight. Her face, hard. *Ever since the day you were born,* she began, *I have tried to protect you. To shield you from disappointment. I have coloured the world around you so that you have only seen the things which were safe and familiar to you. This way I thought that I could keep you safe.* I could see her jaw muscles stiffening and her shoulders tensing as she gripped the chair with her hands. *I don't want us to get hurt.* I reached out to touch her arm, but she pulled away. *No. I don't want to be part of your future. I want to sleep, don't you understand? I am exhausted from trying to shield you from your expectations and now I just want to rest. I have done my best for you and now you don't need me any more. I'm leaving.*

So she did. She left. Her footsteps echoed into the distance, and I heard her no more. There was no coming together of minds, no tearful reunion of disparate personas. There was just silence where she had been. *Thank you for all you tried to do,* I said to the space where she had been. *Thank you and rest now. You deserve it.* I waited. She didn't return. Cautiously at first, I moved over and into the space she had filled for me. I now had a space for my words – new words – a space for my thoughts, a space for me to create a new trance to live. I chose my words carefully from then on, and if ever I heard echoes of her, or if words that she had used crept into my thoughts, instantly and immediately I would replace them. I replaced 'fear' with 'excitement'. I replaced 'cannot' with 'can'. I banished the words 'ought' and 'must' to the outer reaches of my mind because they do not have a place in magic. The Source will not accept these words – and you too will learn to reject them as you heal.

Just before going to sleep tonight, enter your trance by counting down from 300 to zero, using each out breath to time each number as you count down. When you reach zero, you can find yourself at the top of the stone steps once again.

Keep walking until you reach the end of the steps and find yourself back in the beautiful, peaceful, natural landscape which you have already visited. Feel the peace of this place welcoming you home as you look around, and become aware of the colours of the landscape this time. As before, you are going to head towards the river, and find a place to sit down. Watch the river moving, and be aware of the sunlight playing on its surface. Let this sight calm you. As you sit, you become aware of the presence of a figure close by. Invite them to come and sit beside you. This is your inner critic. You have never actually invited them to spend time with you before and they may be wary of your invitation. In the past they would just invade your thoughts, intrude when you didn't want them. You know their voice and their words. This time I want you to ask them to talk. Let their negative words flow out, just as the river flows, but this time, instead of the words hurting you they are carried away by the flow of the river. Allow your inner critic to say all the negative things they think. You may not even consciously register the words, and that is fine. Let them talk until they have no more to say. When it is over, I want you to tell your inner critic that there is no more space in your inner reality for their negativity, and if they want to continue to live then they will have to change their words from negative to positive. If they are prepared to do this, in return you tell them that you will listen to them in future, and that you will not push them away. If they fall back into the old, negative way of talking to you, you will not be able to hear them any more, they will fade further into the past and eventually you will no longer be able to hear them anyway. Offer them life in exchange for their support. Offer them freedom in exchange for their encouragement. This is the deal. There is no negotiation. Change or they become history to be caught up in the mandala of your DreamTime and no longer allowed space or time in your inner reality.

Tell your inner critic that you understand that they have your best interests at heart, that they meant well and you are grateful for their attentions. Understand this, and give them space if they agree to change form. Your inner critic can become your inner coach, helping you change the words of power in your own head.

Do not worry if you find this hard, or even if your inner critic does not respond to you straightaway. It will happen in your sleep and in your dreams, and you will notice how you find yourself changing negative thoughts for positive ones. It will happen.

Rest for a while by the river, and now return to the stairs, and as you walk up the stairs you can still be aware of the presence of the inner critic, but now it feels softer, more friendly – changed. You can acknowledge that this part has tried to protect and shield you, and you may want to give them a new name. No longer critic, but maybe coach – or even friend.

When you return to the top of the stairs you can open your eyes.

As before, if you want to note down your thoughts and feelings about this, do it in your special book now.

Thoughts are the first and the last freedom. Being free and able to express yourself fully and without criticism within your own mind liberates you, no matter where you are or what is happening around you. When you feel safe in your own mind you can allow your power words and phrases to take shape and form in the world around you. You will create a new life trance which will encompass more than yourself. You will be able to bring others into it, creating belief and trust. This is your new reality, and you can and will start to make your imagined world move beyond the confines of your thoughts and into the world around you. Whatever you create with your power words you will begin to find signs of around you. By entrancing yourself with strong and effective power words you will shape the world to your desires. And the very air that surrounds you becomes your atmosphere for change; that which you create around you will be extensions of your thoughts. As you start to grow in strength you will also learn how to move the air around you and project freedom and hope.

For it is in that space between waking and sleeping, where the essence of the Source lies. Everything you have ever known, dreamed or imagined – it is all here. All the light and, more significantly, the darkness between the light. This is the habitation of thoughts that thread you to the world around you with your beliefs about reality. All of the self-imposed limitations which you believed to be reality exist in this space, and none of them is *real* unless you choose to believe in them. In the Waning Moon you can allow the damaged thoughts to flow away from you, carried by the lunar tide.

CHAPTER 16

Dream Time – Dark Moon

TTT

Trance

Mother writes:

Your third eye sees in three directions
Gone before and now and hereafter
An eye for within, an eye for without, an eye for
    DreamTime
Unified thus envisioned now in one for all dimensions
    three.

In the darkness of the DreamTime you exist purely as thought. Unadulterated by matter your experience is clear and untainted. You can learn to fly. As you now understand, DreamTime forms the space between the outer and inner reality and exists as the thinnest barrier between the two. It contains your boundary. The DreamTime removes that which does not fit your inner reality, and allows you to fully sense your environment in a way that will reinforce your way of believing. The boundary therein can be as a halo, or a barbed-wire fence, acting as a light on your path or forming a seemingly impenetrable barrier to your connection to the Source depending on whether you acknowledge that the choice is now yours and you choose to connect to it in those moments between waking and sleeping each morning. There is nothing to believe or disbelieve here. Your connection with the magic within you is all the stronger because this space allows you the freedom to create.

I was in my seventh year. A silent, small and rather odd child, given to singing when in motion and silence when at rest. Conversation with children bored me, and with adults confused me. Too many different languages. Too many different layers of meaning in their words and actions. During that summer, I was taken on a day trip to visit Boggle Hole, a natural tourist attraction on the north Yorkshire coast. I rode on the lap of Auntie Doris in a black bullet of a sidecar, while Uncle Arthur sat astride the beautiful Triumph motorbike which came out only on Sunday afternoons in summer. Auntie Doris was round and pink, and smelled of French Fern talcum powder. Uncle Arthur dressed in leathers and a black pudding-basin helmet striped front-to-back in red and black, topped off with fighter pilot goggles. The leather strap of the goggles bit deep into his skin and made a seemingly permanent ridge around his head. They were both in their sixties then, and because they were not blood relatives, I loved them all the more because of the time they spent with me. They were happy for me to be silent, and gave me space and time to devour books in their home.

Just as they seemed to find nothing strange about me, so I found nothing odd in the fact that she would dress for a day out at Royal Ascot, complete with lace gloves and grand picture hat, while he dressed for a day strutting his stuff in the Ace Café, Park Royal with all the other bikers. I suppose you would call them an odd couple, but they showed me love and I saw only that. That's the way of the child. They only see the love which you give to them, not your oddness. A day out with them was always an adventure. This particular July day it was sunny and the sky was blue and empty of clouds, and we parked the bike in a field above Boggle Hole, overlooking Robin Hood's Bay. I remember it being windy. For that matter I remember most of my childhood as windy.

We ate a proper picnic from a wicker hamper, and drank sickly-sweet tea from a Thermos flask. There is something about the taste of tea from a Thermos, a plastic aftertaste not unpleasing. After lunch they lay down to rest side by side on the red tartan rug while I ran down to the beach to explore the Hole itself. How to describe it? Sitting in the rock facing the beach it is an odd formation. The view from within the cave is that of a black rock picture frame with the sea as its portrait. From outside it is monolithic and prehistoric. I suppose I should have been frightened, but I could hear music within, and like the children of the Pied Piper I was drawn into the cave.

There was a fire and music. Someone was playing a recorder and I could hear a drum. Everyone seemed happy and in motion. Just people being alive. People dancing, smiling, playing. The fire was smoky but people were laughing and ululating. I stood at the mouth of the cave, watching. A tiny, neat Midwich Cuckoo silhouetted by the daylight without the cave. I felt no fear, just a distant curiosity. A young woman danced her way out of the cave towards me, and asked me how old I was. I held up seven fingers to her outstretched face. 'Seven!' she called to the others and they followed her to surround me, spiralling and swaying. She started to trace a circle around me, and the others trod it too. I stayed motionless, a statue of seven years amidst the dancing earth people. The music grew louder as the drummer and piper moved to the mouth of the cave, and I stood still. The dancers moved faster and faster, and raised their arms to the sky. My eyes followed skyward, and I watched the moon rise in the still blue sky. They raised a cone of power around me and I watched the silvery lunar orb of the moon caught and encircled by their hands. I could have stayed there for ever. In that moment I felt the earth and the sky and the moon within me. I was completely safe and connected in a way that I had never experienced before.

I know now that at that moment I existed only in the DreamTime, and that in this state anything was possible. It wasn't a thought, but a complete knowing. I felt it coursing in my blood and causing my heart to race. In this moment the true meaning of what it was to be alive came into me. I could take what I needed and leave what I chose. The DreamTime was infinite in that moment and the knowledge of infinite possibility held me in its sway. In the silence of the ending, I could feel the world come back in to claim me. I could see the sky and hear the sea again. Dogs barked at the surf, and I felt the rush of cold air surrounding me. My breathing returned hard and fast and I ran back to where my aunt and uncle now stood, silhouetted by the sky, side by side by sidecar, for all the world like American Gothic transported to the north coast of England. They never asked what I had been doing – why should they? – and I never told. Magic summoned me on that day and I pulled it around me like a cloak and took it to be the most natural feeling in the world. I closed off the memory safely until Mother opened the door once more, and the new chaos embraced me again to take me to another place.

It is time for you to awaken fully to the power of your DreamTime, so you can know the magic is real and can penetrate beyond your thoughts and into the world around you. This will be both your layer of protection and your creating space. It is time to acknowledge its role in the magic which you will create, time to understand its purpose, and time to nourish it with access to your dreams. As children DreamTime is a real and active force in our lives. It shapes the world we choose to exist within. It allows us to be creative without placing ourselves in danger. As we grow, and society reminds us of our roles and responsibilities, we forget about the DreamTime, and live in the outer world, and the magic recedes from us like an ebb tide. We allow ourselves to live in a world shaped by others – a world in which our dreams seem remote and unachievable. It is time to open your mind to the possibilities around you, and within you. DreamTime is your way in, and your way out of the monochrome life into one which is rich in Technicolor. A life where magic is real and anything is possible for you.

In the space between waking and sleeping, reality is what you dream it to be. The reality outside your mind, the reality of buildings and people and rivers and other things exists whether you interact with it or not, just as you have a deep reality within you which is so personal, so unique, that no language could ever describe it to another soul. All the creatives know this road. Dali would artificially create DreamTime by napping with an outstretched hand and a spoon resting on one finger, and a plate on the floor beneath it. When the spoon clattered down onto the plate he would put the ideas which came to him down on paper. Einstein described this as a time of visions: 'I rarely think in words at all,' he said. When Mendeleev put together the periodic table of chemical elements – a revolutionary concept at the time – it came to him in a dream – including all the *missing elements*. You see, when you enter DreamTime you may not see the whole picture, but you will be able to identify the gaps – the spaces which you need to fill to complete the picture – to make the magic happen. The creatives and scientists who embrace magic are those who step out of the definitions of current reality and create their own. So many of the innovators, those who created new concepts and abstract connections, did so in the DreamTime. You now have your own personal connections, and it is up to you how you use them, and you can be assured that you are in good company when you do.

Now is the time for you to make your connection with the DreamTime open to expand *beyond* the confines of your mind. It is time to create a doorway to allow the magic to flow freely and safely. Until now you have been training yourself to enter DreamTime each morning when you have woken to the light in the morning. This time you are to enter it in trance, and understand the power of your self as experienced in your inner reality. Your own self will become the doorway between inner and outer realities, and things seen, felt and heard in the inner world will now be seen, felt and heard in the outer world. You will start to project the magic outwards, beyond yourself, and will soon be ready to allow it to be carried beyond your experience by other people around you.

Just before going to sleep tonight, enter your trance by counting down from 300 to zero, using your out breath to time each number as you count down. When you reach zero, find yourself at the top of the stone steps once again. The steps are solid rock, worn by the footsteps of the others who came this way before.

Keep walking until you reach the end of the steps and find yourself back in the beautiful, peaceful, natural landscape which you have already visited. Feel the peace of this place surrounding you as you look around. Become aware of the many textures of this natural landscape.

This time, just wander around the magical landscape. Become aware of all the things in the landscape that you know to exist in the outer world. Trees, mountains, rivers, fields – and you. Become aware of your body in this space, how you move and feel. In this inner space you have another existence, and this existence is just as real as your other reality. As in the DreamTime, inner and outer reality can connect. In this landscape you are as real as you wish to be, and you can truly be yourself, just as this landscape has reality – a form which you gave it. It is unique to you. It is time now to move this version of your experience into the outer world. So from now on, every time you see a tree or a river or a mountain, or anything which exists in this landscape, your inner reality will connect with it in the outer world. You start to recognise that you have changed, and the world around you is changing too. You begin to notice the magic of coincidences happening around you. The patterns of change become obvious as your eyes adjust to see the possible realities. The inner you starts to respond, and the magic grows. Don't 'try' to make the connections; they will come to you naturally throughout the coming days. Each time you connect it will strengthen your ability to make the magic happen around you.

You are here to seek the doorway between these two realities, and that doorway is formed out of your senses. You are the doorway. As you experience your own thoughts in this space, so you become able to carry your inner world into the outer world. You are the doorway to creation. Just as seeing or experiencing trees or flowers or mountains when you are out and about will create the energy to link into your inner space, so you, yourself are the doorway to both worlds. By fully seeing, hearing and feeling your surroundings and making the connections within, you blend inner and outer reality and start to mould the world around you as you want it to be. As before do not 'try' to make things happen, just go with the flow of the worlds and experience the events which happen as the doorway opens you up to new experiences.

Rest for a while in the landscape of your inner world and allow yourself to make the connections you need to bring your inner self safely into the world around you. The daily morning DreamTime will strengthen the doorway – and allow it to let your dreams become reality. You can now allow yourself to get excited. The magic is happening to you.

Return to the stairs only when you are ready, and walk up to the top as before.

When you return to the top of the stairs you can open your eyes.

When you feel ready, you can rest a moment and think about this experience. For the last time formally, take up your special book and pen and write down your feelings about the thought of *you* making magic real in your life. Write down what magic you want to see happening around you. Paint the picture of this future with your words. Write everything that comes into your mind.

You will notice that each time you have entered the trances you have taken ever more control. Allow yourself the freedom to explore your inner landscape beyond my words and instructions. You are the master here, and you are free to experience these events in the best way for you. Nothing is prescribed or proscribed here. There are no rules, only guidance.

Mother writes:

The deluge came to purify the earth
Hercules cheats death with his labours
Only through action will life flourish
Flood tide cleanses minds, let it take its tithe.

Closure Ritual

Open the circle. Light your candle and meditate on the candle flame. Allow one of your daydreams to float out into the flame. Let it remain there while you close your eyes and think about this daydream. Let your mind wander now. When you are ready, open your eyes and draw the daydream out of the flame and let it flow beyond the flame. Let it flow out of the room if you wish. Notice now how differently you feel. Notice how much more *real* it feels. You will meet the daydream again, but this time in the outer reality. Extinguish the flame and close the circle.

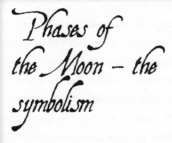

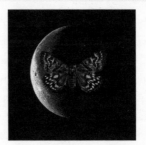

Phases of the Moon – the symbolism

Waning Moon

The final phase of significance is the Waning Moon, personified by the Crone aspect of the Goddess, and it is a time when the tide moves away, draws back and leaves an empty beach. It follows the preparation of the Maiden, the fulfilment of the Mother, and now she comes into her own. It is a time to release and banish, to break patterns.

The strength of the Crone comes from her knowledge and wisdom, and an understanding of the darkness and needs of others. It is a time of self-awareness. This is a time when you release yourself from fear and pain. A time when you recognise your strengths and your limitations, and a time when there are no more games to be played. The Crone sees everything, and in her light you are reduced to your essential self. This is the self who is aware of their own death, and through this has discovered the magic of life.

This is the Moon phase in which you will let go of the things which have not worked for you during this lunar cycle. Let them go, and free yourself from regret. It was not the right time.

This is a phase in which you can grieve. You are allowed to experience the pain of loss and can let yourself be sad or regretful. Remember this is a phase and it will pass, but we all need time on occasion to mourn. It is healthy and will allow you to grow and develop.

This is the phase of the teacher within us. We are at the most connected to our guides at this time, and you can go to your guide at this time with questions and request answers, or signs of which way to move forward.

CHAPTER 17

Epiphany
– Waxing Moon

‡

Trance

Mother writes:

The light of Revelation shines forth from your third
   eye
You own your inner space
Time to make manifest and disturb the air betwixt
   oneself and t'other
Time to enlighten, time to shine
Time to make the magic thine.

Take a few moments to think about your life. Think about the
times when you had failed to make a stand, whether it was
for yourself, or for the other. Times when you walked past
the homeless man, and hoped that they would not call out to
you, times when you threw away a request for charity, times
when you ignored a cry for help when it was inconvenient to

you. For each of us these memories prick at our conscience. Acknowledge it. You are human, and part of our make-up is that of self-preservation. It does not make you a bad person, but the fact that you have registered these times in your memory means that they have some emotional content for you. They do not sit well with you and this is why you can still remember them. I ask you to allow yourself to remember them now because it is time for you to move the fulcrum along so you can get balance back, and so you can and will never feel the need to feel this discomfort again. I am not asking you to help everyone, always – that would be destructive to you and it would not help – but I will guide you to a space where you can reach out willingly, and in a way that will enrich and nourish your life – not diminish it.

Now is the time for you to open your mind to the phenomenal power of thought. Especially when those thoughts are given shape and amplified in the minds of others, as you will have the potential to do when you are connected to the Source.

This is the time to open your mind to other ways of feeling and thinking, philosophy, religion, travel, education. Time to open the doors in you and move through into the realm of infinite possibilities. Time to stop blaming yourself for what you could have done and start healing yourself by making things happen for others. These acts are the fuel of magic.

To move freely to this stage it helps to have an epiphany to crystallise this knowledge and to make it real. Epiphany is the moment of insight – the time when the inner world, DreamTime, and the outer world can be seen in the same light. This is the moment when you start to project DreamTime onto the world around you. Your inner reality takes form and substance. You start to shape your surroundings to your needs and desires and it all comes together. It is like a magic eye picture at the moment you see it emerging from the patterns. It comes to each of us in different ways – some more dramatic than others.

This moment of realisation as to the extraordinary phenomenon that is life came to me a long time ago as I watched life leave a vibrant, healthy body I held in my arms and I couldn't stop from going. I was twenty years old, and had made my home within a group of merry outsiders. I was a live-in bar attendant in a gay club in one of the shabbier immigrant areas of London. This wasn't exactly a safe place to live, for many reasons, not least of which was that it was 1983 and the spectre of Aids, which had just hit the UK, hung over the country, and gay-bashing was at its height. The owners of the club had given me a home when I needed it, and I gave them my love and loyalty. These people became my family. Not only those who gave me a home and a job, but the others who came there to belong. Not everyone was gay there, but all who came had their own 'differences', whether these were political or sexual, religion, size or age or dressing preference. All were welcome provided you were prepared to enter Dorothy's kingdom of Oz and you danced to the beat of the disco drum. I loved it there, and allowed my own idiosyncrasies to take form. I felt at home and safe. Then came the night when I met death.

Fights in the street where I lived were not uncommon on a Saturday night. This one was different. It rumbled like a storm, and grew more violent as the night went on. Just noise, shouting from outside, and something soggy landed on one of the windows. We ignored it. These things usually abated without fuel. We took little notice.

There were two worlds on that street that night, and neither of them was Kansas. I remember seeing the sequins on the drag act's gown sparkling in the light of her cigarette as she waited to come on stage. Red lips topped with a bouffant blond wig. A strange image vividly imprinted on my brain cells. The sounds outside subsided, and the music thumped its way through the night and I carried on with my work. It got late, and I don't know how I found myself outside when it happened, but I watched a tide of men pour over the solitary boy as he left the club behind me and they dragged him across the road, leaving him bloodied, half on the road, half on the pavement. I ran across to him and knelt by his body. I moved so he could rest his head on my lap. Behind me I could hear shouts as people came out of the club and ran over to where I knelt stroking the boy's hair. He wasn't moving. The blood had seeped through his – until then pristine white – cap-sleeved T-shirt, and turned it black and heavy, the texture of a rubber sheet. I felt others standing mutely around me pull off their own T-shirts and hand them to me. I tried to staunch his wound with the cloth, but as I did I felt his body convulse and blood bubble from his mouth. He went still. His blind eyes looked up at me, and I howled out his pain to the Waning Moon lighting the street that night.

Funny, isn't it, what sticks in your memory. I don't remember seeing the Moon before or since in that street. That nameless boy died there, that night, in that dirty street. He couldn't have been more than eighteen years old. Just a boy who had been out for a good time. Just a boy. And now he was dead. Killed by prejudice and fear and ignorance. When the police came and the ambulance had taken his body away, I returned inside. I don't remember the sound of any music, but felt the bodies around me part and create a path as I walked through the crowd. A parody of a prophet with my bloodied hands held stiff. Palms held forward in supplication shouting the words which I couldn't voice. And all the while the savage red of Lily's sequined dress scintillated in the light of the mirror ball. No Pearl and Dean fanfare for the dead boy – not even a name. The unknown soldier in the war of prejudice and hate.

I went upstairs and showered. I let the water burn my skin and my tears mix with the water. So much blood. Too much blood. I cried out of fear for myself, for my friends, and I shivered and cried because I didn't even know his name and he had died in my arms.

He was just a boy. It could just as easily have been any of us. I, and the others, talked about feeling guilty that we had not gone out sooner, had not tried to stop it from happening. It made no sense. I knew in my heart of hearts that there was nothing I could have done then, but I could stand up and fight from now on. And I did. And I still do. It will never be the easy option. You will rarely get praise for it, and there may be times when you wish you could just give it up. Doing the right thing doesn't make you popular, but I no longer had a choice after that day. I had held another human being as life left them, and in that moment I made my choice to fight ignorance, fear and prejudice. There isn't always a clear, right answer, either. I can only now do what I *feel* to be right, rather than turning over the magazine page on the horrific images of women damaged in war, or turning my back on the homeless man. This knowledge became the grit in my oyster for me to try to make something beautiful in the world. Mother now guides me to be true to myself in this, and not swayed by money or fame or kudos – but reminds me of that boy's death – his death in exchange for my epiphany. This knowledge pushes me to remember why it is important to do what you *can* to make changes happen in this world. We are participants in life, not observers, and I know it could just as easily have been me who died out in the street that night. Mother held up the mirror to my soul and showed me its true colour. We are all connected one with the other and to turn my back on him would be to turn my back on myself. Then, many years later when I had fully connected with the Source of magic within me, I truly knew that there is no other way forward but to fight for those who do not have a voice.

Now it is your time to make that choice. There may be no one clear epiphany for you, but the knowledge is already within you about what is the right thing to do. You are ready to listen to that which is right from within you, and to respond. This is part of the magic which will change the world. Let go of the regrets, the things which you wish you had done and didn't do, and the things which you did do and now regret having done. It is time to learn from the past, and make the future a different place. It is time to stand up for those who do not have a voice or a home. We live on one huge and potentially beautiful world, but with so much darkness and inequality. This is your time to shift the balance and make a difference. Move the fulcrum so the scales even up. You will get your chance for redemption, if you feel this is needed, and you will know what to do this time. You cannot change the past and make it right, but you can change the future, not just for yourself, but for all of us. Little by little, step by step. It is time to push your dreams for life out from your inner space, through the DreamTime and into the world around you. It is time to express your dreams and make the magic happen with your actions for others.

Just before going to sleep tonight, enter your trance by counting down from 300 to zero as usual. Find yourself at the top of the stone steps once again. The steps are solid rock, worn by the footsteps of the others who came this way before. You have no burdens. Your way is clear and brightly lit. You are now familiar with this journey.

Keep walking until you reach the end of the steps and find yourself, for the last time, back in the beautiful, peaceful, natural landscape where you can feel safe. Feel the peace of this place surrounding you as you look around and allow yourself to take in the whole scene around you.

Find any place where you can make yourself comfortable, and lie down there. Close your eyes, and be aware of the light from the sun as it penetrates through your eyelids. Be aware of it just as you are now becoming used to waking to the light in the morning, and spending time in that space between waking and sleeping. This is your time and space – remember this.

As you lie there, I want you to allow yourself to let one image come into your mind, an image which you would ordinarily push away. This is an image of a starving child, or a beaten animal, an image which reminds you of all the injustice and darkness in the world. You are strong enough to deal with this now.

When this image is in your mind – let one thought come to you. *From now on I will not look away – I will be your voice.* Let this thought ring out in your mind.

Take the child or the animal somewhere safe in this dreamscape where they can heal.

Now spend time alone.

Spend time here, and allow your inner mind to make the connections you need to make these thoughts of change real to you. From now on, in your morning DreamTime, you can allow your daydreams space to find their way out into the world. Allow your dreams to spill out into reality. Look for ways of making change happen – listen out for them – feel them happening around you as you grow towards the Source of your own magic. Know the voice of justice. Become the voice of change.

Return to the stairs when you are ready, and walk up to the top as before.

When you return to the top of the stairs you can open your eyes.

Write down your thoughts and feelings now. Write down the actions too. You are stronger now – stronger than you thought or felt before, and you are now ready to initiate the change and to make it real. You are ready to connect with the Source.

Mother writes:

Betwixt and between now thou art
Know ye this
All things on heaven and earth can be for good or ill
We each have choice, we all have free will
Use it well, make it count
Evil ignored is evil spread out.

Closure Ritual

Open the circle. Light your candle and take a moment to meditate on the flame. Allow the regrets you had about things which you wish you had done, could have done but didn't do, take form as one thought and float this thought into the flame. Close your eyes and forgive yourself for these things, and make a promise to yourself that in future you will do what you know to be the right thing. Open your eyes and thank the flame for absorbing your regrets and giving you light. Extinguish the flame and close the circle.

As the next few weeks progress, you will find an opportunity to get involved in something which will help other people around you. You may volunteer your time, or give money, or skills or knowledge, but in this act of giving you heal yourself. Do not force it. The opportunities will come to you, and you will be ready to accept your connection with those around you. You will experience an incredible sense of peace when you do this, all the more so when you do not feel the need to feed your ego by telling others. This is about you and your relationship with the Source, not about self. It will come, and you will be amazed at how much you gain from these connections.

CHAPTER 18

Synergy – Full Moon

⫼

Rite

Mother writes:

As Ruth the Moabite found favour in the eyes of Boaz
Let it be known that a stranger gives kindness unto
  you.
Earned in secret, given in silence
This gift will change your life for ever.

While I was changing, what had happened to all my dreams, all the things which I wanted to happen magically? Before – before connecting to the Source that is, before I had changed – I thought that the magic would involve me asking for things to happen, and they would appear. Even further back, when I still denied Mother's words, I had thought that if I worked hard and consistently then I would get what I wanted – no magic required, just effort and focus. I had thought I could manipulate the world to my preferences by sheer willpower alone. No feelings required. Now I had come to recognise that sensing the magical is a vital component in extraordinary change, but it doesn't appear just because you *want* it. You have to create it and then nurture it. True magic gives you the vision and the energy to see the world in a different way, and to truly be one with the Source of all magic. So, while I was changing, the world around me was changing with me, and my dreams were taking shape in reality. Seemingly random events came together. Connections between events which I created in the DreamTime moved into the outer world, and I found myself in the right place at the right time. People I thought I knew brought different things to my table, and I allowed them to be part of my change. This was the strangest part of the lesson for me – that by changing my inner landscape, and putting that change around me by my actions, I created the magical atmosphere for synergy. I was making magic *for those around me*, and the magic came back to me amplified many, many times.

It happened like this. I would give my time to someone, and while I was with them I found myself talking about the magic, and what was happening to me. I talked about my dreams and my plans. I shared without fear that the sharing would somehow diminish my dreams. It was ironic. Before (in that now distant and ice-strewn country of the past), I would not have told anyone of my dreams, for fear of them being stolen, or that my plans would upset them, or that by telling someone I would somehow put a hex (how ironic!) on it happening. I soon learned that people would listen to me if I was open with them and showed how it had helped me change. I opened myself up to receive gifts, something which I had found difficult or impossible before. I only accepted the gifts which I *needed*, those which moved me forward. I accepted nothing more. I no longer feared the capacity of others to help me, and the relationships in which that placed me. Most often the people I helped were people who were in no position to help me back in practical ways – they needed my help, and that was *why* I was with them, but their love and enthusiasm – the kind words and the good wishes which they gave to me – were like food to a starving man. They fuelled me and gave texture and colour to my magic. Their wishes for my success sent out to the universe made the magic stronger, and my dreams became reality. Those who believed themselves in no position to help me ended up helping me most of all. They helped me understand that the true nature of magic is in the giving and sharing of it.

So, in order for this to work for you there is one simple fact. *You must give to those around you with no expectation or desire for something in return.* You must give purely because it will benefit the other person. The more effort or energy, time or money you put into this, *with a good heart,* the greater the Source of magic grows within you. At first you may find it irritating, or time-consuming, or simply too much effort – but stay with it. You will get back whatever you put into these relationships and times, but the likelihood is that it will not come directly from the person to which you gave some of yourself.

When I started on this road and gave my time and expertise to other people at no charge, and (I felt at the time) considerable inconvenience and effort to myself, I puffed myself up with pride at what a good person I was. I couldn't resist telling other people what I was doing. I wanted payback, ego-payback – I wanted praise. Wrong, wrong, wrong! The Source ran dry very quickly, and I found myself falling back into old patterns and thought processes where I became needy and unreasonable, feeling trapped by my new obligations. Mother's words came to me: *Everything you do is a choice ...* So I chose to help others. I gave them my respect and my full attention. The more difficult they were, the more effort I put in – and it worked. The magic came back, a trickle at first, and then a flood. My self-respect grew as I realised that I was making magic happen for others, and this feeling was the right feeling. It fed my spirit and my soul, and my ego had no place in this equation any more. Odd coincidences started to occur; someone I had never met but who had heard of the work I was doing, brought me the gift of a name. This name gave me time and information, and I made connections. The dreams started to become reality. Nothing that I did from this time – provided I did it with an open heart and no expectation of personal gain – was wasted. At first, I needed to keep reminding myself that everything I was doing was a choice. I had made this decision to put magic out into the world and to make my journey to the Source a real and practical statement about how I would live my life. This was an emotional tithe, and I was happy to pay it for what it had brought to me. The magic continued to grow. The coincidences and connections magnified, and extraordinary events became commonplace for me. I saw them in the DreamTime, had lived them in my inner reality, and now they were appearing all over the outer reality, like wild flowers – and it was wonderful. Others around me were starting to see it and to be attracted to it. They wanted to know about the magic. And, because they asked, I shared the knowledge and my journey with them. I shared Mother's words with a select few, and the magic grew beyond me. The Web of Wyrd reached further and further afield. I was happiest in the sharing of this gift. Besides, I *had* promised Mother . . .

I realised in those moments that magic was not something in which you asked for things for yourself, it was something you created for others. Mother had taught me that *magic is something which happens when you are not looking – it happens in the corner of your eye, not in front of them.* And all the while I was changing and connecting to the Source, all the time I was pushing my dreams and hopes through the space between my inner reality and the outside world, using myself as the doorway. Those dreams and hopes were moving beyond me and connecting with others – others who could, and would, make those dreams into reality.

And so through this process I found love. Self-love. Self-respect. A true and honest appreciation of myself which opened me to care about myself without guilt or a need to justify myself. This came with an understanding and recognition of myself with all my flaws. I had learned, through my Mother guide, to listen to the inner voice which was moving me forward on the path to the Source. I didn't always enjoy the advice, nor did I always feel comfortable to act on the suggestions she made. I had finally learned that it is not important *who* is right, but *what* is right, and I didn't need to fight the whole world any more. I learned humility. And before you think I had disappeared up my own fundament, let me tell you that there are times when I enjoy a good old blow on my own trumpet, but this is more for old times' sake than any real enjoyment I get out of puffing myself up. It is only a habit now, and one I am comfortable to take off and leave behind.

Once I had learned to love myself, and give due respect to my own efforts, love with another person found me. To be honest, it wasn't as straightforward a journey as I would have liked it to be (but perhaps this is the whole point!) and it wasn't blistering, passionate, swept-off-my-feet, Mills & Boon romance, by any means. We got to know each other as friends. First came liking, then laughter, then respect, followed by a deep understanding. I learned to love a man who has no need to tell everyone his skills and abilities. He is secure in himself. Not at all what I expected, and everything I needed. Mother was spot on with this one. After learning to share who I really was, with this man, there came a love the like of which I have never experienced before, and a passion which continues to grow. I now have an appreciation for life shared, which can only come when you are comfortable enough to trust yourself to trust completely in another person. I now have a person in my life to love, and who loves me in return. There are no dark corners in our relationship, nor are there games or power play. This love came only when I was able to be honest with myself. Only then did I find and connect with a man who was secure in himself and not only willing but able to connect with another person. Only once I had found who I was, was I prepared to share that with another. We always have something to talk about. We can spend twenty-four hours a day in each other's company and still be at peace. We can be apart and not needy. We can be silent together, and truly feel for one another in success or sadness. With this relationship I got the happy ending – or happy beginning, as I prefer to call it. We married for love and by candlelight, with family and friends around us. Friends. I had forgotten how vital they were to my wellbeing. Friends were something else I had sacrificed in my obsession with taking on the world. The magic brought them back to me, and I met other new people to whom I am now proud to give the name of friend.

In all of this the never-to-be-neglected ingredient is connection. Connections between brain cells, connections between thoughts and ideas, connections between inner and outer realities, connections with the world around you and the people in it. Magic does not happen in a vacuum, it needs connections to move around. The creation of these connections requires confidence and honesty. I stopped being afraid of success and of other people. I now allow both into my reality. For you, you are now in a place and time to connect with your roots and the power of your ancestors, allowing you to appreciate the lives they led to give you life now. Reconnect with those you care about. Go out now and connect with those you love and tell them that you love them. Make your words count. Write to them if you can't bring yourself to say the words. Connect with life. This is also the time to find the others, the kindred. You can use the web and become a member of the Facebook group **The Source: A Manual of Everyday Magic**, or tweet me and other like-minded people on Twitter, or browse the website suggestions at the end of this book for places to get involved. You can and you will find your own ways of connecting with open-hearted people. Seek out the others who are on their own journey, and feel free to meet me again in the heart of the Web.

The connections which you took time to form each morning

have now formed connections in the outer world. You are not the first to do this, and you will not be the last. Take the last step to moving magic out into the wider world and connect now to Mother Moon. Harness her power for the fullest expression of the magic.

Closure Ritual

In this ritual you allow all the fragments of your story to be pulled together in the outer reality which surrounds you, and for you – wonderful reader – to become one with yourself. No more limits, no more lost pieces, no more dark corners. Complete and ready.

This ritual will also allow you to give thanks to the Source for making you welcome. Give thanks to all the people and all of the events in your life that have come together to make up who you are today. The good and the bad, they are all part of you. In this ritual you can accept yourself for who you are and for what you have done in your life and you can know that you are ready to welcome true magic into your life. You are now ready to own your future, and ready to feel that you deserve magic in your life. Your desire to crush or ignore it will be burned in the spirit of the candle flame which you are about to light.

This is the time to thank the Source as it comes to meet you. Open the circle. Light your candle. Invite the essence of all those from your ancestor corner and all those who have come into your life through the magic, and invite them into the gentle flame of the candle. Watch it flicker before you.

It is time for you to know that the candle flame has its own life. Fire is an elemental. And, as you watch it move you can feel the elemental spirit of the flame. You can feel its power. It is a power to destroy or create, as are all the elementals around you. From now on, whenever you light a flame for ritual you are asking the elemental within this flame to summon the ancestors and those who love you to participate in your rituals and to support you in your journey to the Source. Watch the flame flicker, grow larger and smaller as these spirits come and go during your ritual, and in your future rituals. As they come and go they bring gifts with them. They can bring support, benevolence, self-belief, kindness, selflessness. They will bring to you exactly what you need at the time. You may wish to silently name the gifts they bring to you as you watch the flame. Thank them as you do.

Spend some time with the elemental flame. Close your eyes and see the glow of the flame once more. Thank the elemental flame for helping you to focus the magic of your inner world, and project it outwards.

Open your eyes and blow out the candle flame.

Close the circle and cleanse your hands. Open the window and stand up. You bring air, fire, earth and water together in this ritual. You synergise the energy of all of them into a simple act.

Mother writes:

So did Ruth in the cornfield knew Boaz' gifts,
Bake your own bread now you shift,
The choice is clear, this much I contrive
Choose ill and remain as one barely alive. Choose well
and with Mother Moon's embrace you thrive.

Lammas

This festival is celebrated at the end of July or beginning of August in the northern hemisphere, and the end of January or beginning of February in the southern.

This is a time of enjoying the first fruits of your labour, of prosperity and continued success. Lammas is a time to reflect on your hard work, and offer gifts to others in the form of money or help. It is a time to reflect, to rest and enjoy pleasurable pursuits. Lammas celebrations involve feasting and sharing your gifts with those who have shared your work. The making and sharing of bread is particularly symbolic at this time.

Lammas is also the time to give yourself rest and time to re-create your goals. By giving gifts now without expectation of return you will maximise your connection with the Source. Best of all, give anonymously for these gifts will reward you a hundred times over. These are the gifts that will keep you warm through the winter months, and they form a different type of harvest from the one that you have just reaped. Gifts given at this time are seeds sown by you and will be reaped as a spiritual harvest throughout the dark winter months.

Finally it is a time for reflection on all you have done since last Lammas, and all you intend to do until the next. It is a time to allow yourself to register regrets as recognition that you will do things differently in future. It is a time to preserve good things, both the fruits of the harvest and positive ways of thinking and acting. It is also a time to say farewell to that which has not added to your abundance, whether this means letting go of certain people, or changing your ways of doing things.

CHAPTER 19

Oneness Combined (the creator) – Full Moon

✠

Rite, Ritual and Trance

Mother writes:

Take liberal heart when the sky fills with night
Satanic spume and the fiery earth taught you man is
   not to fly.
Silence the skies and listen to your heart,
For the black swans are the first to depart.

Final Ritual

Wait until night falls within the seven days of the Full
Moon. Pick the clearest night you can. Go out into the
garden, or the fields, or open the windows wide. It is time
to draw down the Moon and invoke her power to surround
you and become an integral part of your magic. With this
she will become a window on the Source. With bare feet
grounding you, bathe in the light of the Full Moon. Raise

your arms and allow her light to pour through your body. Welcome her into your life wordlessly, for she understands your request. Thank her for sharing her power with you, and feel her respond to you.

When you have completed all you wish to do here, lower your arms, and return indoors. Understand that with this final ritual you are freeing yourself from false constraints, and allowing all that is super within the natural to become part of your life.

Perhaps you still have doubts. Suspicions, maybe. Questions, most certainly. That's fine. I wouldn't blame you. It took a lot of pain and convincing for me to get to the stage of writing this book, and even more agonising before deciding to publish. One of the results of opening up your mind to the possibilities of a new form of reality is that you often seem to have more questions than answers. It doesn't matter because, in formulating the question, you set in motion a train of events that crosses the barrier between inner and outer reality, and the answers will come. They are not always in the form which you initially expected — nor will you always like the answers — but now you are able to sense the answers and are open to choice. For some, the choice is to change nothing, but they are then no longer able to trick themselves, like the fool, into believing that they have no options — that they are helpless prisoners of events. Doing nothing becomes a conscious decision when you have experienced contact with the Source, and you will then recognise that to do nothing is your decision — your inaction itself becomes an active choice.

For most who come into contact with the Source, there is little choice but to change. Small steps at first, gradually accumulating into amazing change. You have the power to be amazing — truly amazing — and the opportunity to make a genuine and absolute difference to the world around you. Just imagine how you are feeling now, and multiply that by the number of people reading this book around the world. Imagine the magic being passed along the Wyrd Web and becoming a living entity, a force for change. A force for good. Yours is now a Bayesian brain*, and you can and will harness the free energy within and make form and structure from the uncertainty around you.

We truly live in interesting times – dramatic times. Times when the shift from the West to the East as the economic powerhouse is inevitable. Do not underestimate the knowledge and understanding of Moon by Eastern cultures. You only need to look at financial trades and lunar cycles in the East to know that there is already an awareness of the power of Sister Moon – and it is an awareness that they are only starting to harness at full capacity. One can always argue that belief in the Moon phases creates a self-fulfilling prophecy – but ultimately does it matter which came first, the Moon's pull or the belief? The result is the same. In the West we have flooded our night sky with light, and hid Sister Moon and the stars in a fog of our own capabilities. Man hid the power of anima magic† from sight, and convinced himself that, in his cleverness, he no longer needed her. We allowed ourselves to forget that she was there, pulling at our emotions, creating space and time for magical events, ready and willing to be harnessed for the benefit of Mother Earth and all her children. Man took the power of numbers from the Moon and moulded them to profit, turning the thirty-three ratios into a sacred text‡. The sky is still seen, read and understood in the stillness of the East. Respect for Mother Moon is strong, and she responds in kind.

For just because Mother Moon has been hidden from sight by the false light of 'civilisation', it does not mean her power is

* The Bayesian brain is a model for the way in which it self-organises. This theory states that when presented with new problems we organise the information statistically, with the result that we predict probabilistically what might happen based on our memory and past experiences.
† Anima magic comes from the female. Like yin (female energy) and yang (male energy), balance between anima and animus is needed for harmony to exist.
‡ Peter Temple, *Magic Numbers: The 33 Key Ratios That Every Investor Should Know.*

diminished, far from it. Her power is there for all those who choose to observe, and Mother Moon can be read in many different ways. She can be read as a sequence in time, she can be read from the events which change in response to her. She can be read in the power of the numbers who believe in her and behave in kind. She can be read as numbers, numbers of power and hidden meaning. And so it is too with any book of power. They can be read in a number of ways, whether it is *Alice's Adventures in Wonderland**, Kaballah texts, books about trees, many, many books, and it is up to you, the reader, what you choose to see within them — what pattern you recognise. You bring the magic to the books, you bring your ability to find meaning for yourself where others would find none.

If you wanted to, you could read this book itself in numbers. You might notice that there are seven trances and know that seven is a fundamental number of the manifest universe and the number which signifies the study of magic. You might read it in Ogham so the trees will shade each chapter with their meaning, read it in acrostics, read it in the comings and goings of the tide. If you think I have got the numbers of the trances wrong, think again. Read the trances and if you counted eight you have counted Death in your total. Death counts as a zero, without which the other numbers do not function. There are a myriad paths to the Source and it does not matter which you choose. Bring to this book *your* own power, *your* knowledge, *your* magic. Make of it what you can and you *will*. Choice will always be yours. Even if you try to ignore her, Sister Moon influences you as a child of Mother Earth, a child of nature. Whether you tread concrete pavements all your life, or you work in the fields, Sister Moon influences you and now you can take control of this influence, and become not just natural, but *supernatural*. It

---

* Dr Charles Dodgson, reverend, mathematician and author of *Alice's Adventures in Wonderland*, was better known as Lewis Carroll. Recent research suggests that he used this story to lambast the newly-discovered quantum mathematics.

is time to take all you have learned, all you have felt, and all you would like to believe but, perhaps, do not yet dare to demand, and step off the well-trodden path and create another one.

This is not only an interesting time in which we live, but an extraordinarily magical one. As we move towards the year 2012 we are entering an era of spiritual awakening, a genuine awareness of nature, its power, and our role in the care of Mother Earth. A time when the earth reminds us of its strength and fury. It is a time when all of the petty dealings of man are thrown into turmoil by nature – drought and floods, volcanoes and earthquakes. A lot is happening out there. We no longer have a choice but to listen and take action. John Petersen, founder of the Arlington Institute says we are at the start of 'megachanges' – the collapse of the banking system, the end of fossil fuels as viable sources of energy, serious climate changes and more. Our world is changing – and it is time to become active in the changes you want to see happen, not just accept the repercussions of current events. In the same way that Ralph Elliott's Wave Principle demonstrated that prices in financial markets swing in response to mood, so does the capacity for an individual to influence changes around them. Believe in what you are attempting to do, and you will influence the mood and feelings of others around you. This is true magic. This is what it means to be connected to the Source – to have an understanding of your own power to make remarkable change happen.

Above all, I am trying to tell you that the experience which you are having when you read this book belongs to you. You can't share it, but you can pass on the effects. Your uniqueness is now part of the pattern of change. You will change the words in this book and give it power way beyond my knowledge and dreams – and with that I fulfil my obligation to her, to Mother Shipton – to put the words out there and to give them the freedom to transform.

So at the end of my journey I went back to my wardrobe and took out the Vivienne Westwood suit. It no longer seemed so stiff and formal. It felt like an old rag doll with not enough stuffing. It wasn't alive any more. I no longer needed it, so I went home to France and carried it out into the garden, and from there followed the path into the wood. I waited quietly until the only light was the Moon, and looking up saw the brightest, fullest Moon caught in the branches of a nearby poplar tree. I gathered fallen twigs imbued with all my fears and doubts about the future, and I made them into a pyre, and lit it. Poor revenant. She lived, she fought, she died. This was a funeral pyre for the Valkyrie I used to be. It was a habit I wore and lived, but no more would I have to decide who lived and died in battle. The war was over and it was time for peace and for the Völva* in me to rise from the phoenix flame. I folded the Vivienne Westwood reverentially and placed it onto the flames, and watched the last remnant of my old life burn away. I stayed until every scrap of cloth burned in the many-hued flame. I stayed until the fire burned to ashes, and when the morning came I returned to the wood and swept the ashes out into the river. One brief season later I returned to the spot and found a tiny elder shoot showing me she was exorcised from my life. The elder took root to give me the healing I needed. I have spent much time in that wood since then. It feeds me and welcomes me, it gives me connection with the earth. I love it there in a way that she would never have understood. Her high heels would have sunk in the mud. She needed concrete under her feet and in her mind. I need the earth and her abstractions. Life is good now – and for me the journey goes on.

But why keep travelling? Surely the journey is over? The fact of the matter is that when you become part of the Source and you fill your days with magic, you understand that standing still is not an option and that the only way to stay poised and

---

* Shamanic seeress. Carrier of a magical wand.

in balance is to move forward. It's like riding a bike! You cannot freeze time and you must not try to freeze magic by attempting to freeze your life in the moments of bliss. Move on. Appreciate yourself and the moments you have lived through. Cherish your soul. Who cares what other people think about you, if you know that you are whole and connected. I don't care about other people's thoughts any more. I do care about their feelings, and that is enough. It took a long time. Too long – but I also know I am still a work in progress. I can now cheer when other people thrive, and I can celebrate myself and my achievements in a way alien to the other me. Life is extraordinary. It is precious. It is wonderful and full of wonder. It is *far* too precious to waste it in front of the television, too precious to wait for others to tell you what to think and feel, too precious to spend it with people who do not nourish you, or in a space which saddens you. The prison door is open. Walk through it. Be free. Be magical.

You are now nearing the end of the journey. This part of it at least. From now on you will make your own way, but this time you are no longer alone. You have your guide and you now know that there are others on the path. It is up to you if you choose to contact them or not. Some prefer to travel a solitary path, others want to meet up with like-minded souls and travel together. Now you have come to this space and time, I want to ask you a question. The question is: on what level did you read this book? Literally? As a metaphor or allegory for our times? As a paradigm? As a piece of literature, a work of magical realism? However you read it I know that you will want to ask a question of me. You want to know if it is true – did I get everything I wanted? That's what everyone wants to know, because if it is, what now? Excellent question, dear reader, and I will answer you as fully as I can. I can tell you that it is true. All of it. Every word on every level. For me, that is, these words are a chronicle. My experience through my senses alone. You see, your experience of this book and the events which lead from it may be events which you experience on one or some of the levels I have described. I wish I could experience them with you, but the story now is yours alone. I got everything that I thought I wanted, and then some. My revelation was that most of it did not matter to me in the way I had thought it would. What mattered in the end was people, and love, and connection. It wasn't about what I *wanted*, more about what I wanted to *give*. What mattered in the end was doing what I knew to be right and not listening to others who told me different things. Through this process I discovered who I truly could be, and I learned to respect and love this person. Yes. It is all true.

I can tell you too that there will be moments for you, and this I do know, when you allow yourself to be suspended and supported within the Source when you will truly experience magic on all four levels. There will be a chord struck in the universe, a blissful harmonic will occur, and everything comes together in that moment. It did for me – and it still does. The feeling is almost impossible to describe, and unattainable if you try too hard. It just happens and you become part of something much greater than yourself. It is like being newborn and ancient simultaneously – existing absolutely in the moment and yet aware of aeons gone by and time still to come. It is like being completely alone in a crowd of people. It is like hearing colours when in the past you only saw them. In these moments I am truly alive – as you will be. As you now can *allow* yourself to be. It is time to live within the Source and make magic happen all around you. The moments of bliss become woven together in harmony with the reality around and within each one of us. These threads then form into a rich carpet complete with flaws so we can appreciate that which is truly perfect.

There is one final trance for you to experience. This time there is no counting, no steps, no inner landscape. This is because the final trance is the one which you are now living and breathing and will continue to live as long as you keep yourself connected to the Source. This is true entrancement. By completing your journey to the Source you are now the creator of your future. You have become the source of your own magic. This final trance state is one of a rich connection with your inner and outer self. One in which you can no longer trick or fool yourself out of success as you used to do. This is the Trance of Life. From this point in time you control your destiny in a very real way. Each day when you wake to the light and choose to spend time in the DreamTime – no matter how short a time that may be – you are reinforcing your personal magic, just as when you go to sleep at night and filter out the events and emotions of your day, you are creating this magical state which then enters your dreams. You are connected with yourself, and now with the Source of that magic itself. It is within you. It is all around and without you. No need for a ritual here. You are breathing the Source of magic. You are at one with the Source. Feel it in the beat of your heart. Understand it now - you are one with the Source.

Look back now to who you were when you started reading this book. I truly hope you have found your way into the Source and become a creature of the supernatural – a magical individual. There is more to life even than you have dreamed of, and more of us dreaming new lives than you can possibly know. You can and will look back into the past, and forward to your future. The past no longer belongs to you, but the future is yours now. You have the tools and the knowledge to live every moment of your life from within the Source of magic, and to feed your own and the magic of others. You are free now to become part of the dream, and make changes happen. Small at first, but then by connecting with others and expanding your magic further into the world around you, you can and you will make amazing change occur. You don't need to believe in magic now – you can believe in yourself and own it. You are one with the Source. Stand within the Source and shine your light on poverty and hate, war and discrimination. Be the change and strike a chord around your world that will join with all the others singing out in harmony for peace, love and justice.

For my part, I thank you. I thank you for meeting me halfway. I thank you for coming on this journey. I thank you for completing these words. Now go out there and live life on Mother Earth and under Sister Moon. You are one with the Source, and are no longer alone.

Your journey onward is now all about you and your future. From now on, you write the book – you have already started, remember. From now on you choose the words of power that go into your special book. You may write poems, simple inspirational phrases, or place images in there. You may put down thoughts, plans and dreams. You may draw or write. I use my book to drill down into words and find deeper magic within when I need a sign. Within the Source right now I find:

Stability,

Ownership,

Understanding,

Righteousness,

Courage and

Empathy, and each time I revisit the word I find others hidden within the letters to inspire and support me through whatever is happening in my life. From now on you will decide the contents of your special book and how you choose to use your knowledge. You make the magic. You have your own book of light and shadows. It will be your recipe book. It will be your guidebook. It will be whatever you need it to be whenever you open it.

From now on you are the author of your book, the architect of your future, the creator of your life.

From this time forward the rites and the rituals are all yours to choose and you will do them where and when you want to do them. The only boundary for you now is to remember to work with the lunar cycles to allow Mother Moon to amplify your work. Dark Moon for understanding, Waxing for preparation, Full for fruition, Waning for letting go. Working within these cycles will give you structure and help you to rein in the chaos and find the structure within. You have found New Chaos Magic – not the Chaos Magic of groups and shifting reality, but the New Chaos of creating your reality on a higher plane, that of an individual new inner reality. As in the hermetic texts, 'As above, so below.' By creating order above in what was the chaos of your inner reality, and defining its parameters in the DreamTime, so you manifest this reality below – in your daily, waking life. Your journey this far was made up of patterns of rituals, punctuation points of rites, and connection with the Source through trance. With all of these you have created a New Chaos – one in which you can see the patterns, and through them you will live the magic. All those coincidences, all those people, all those events, most of them are happening now because you are making them happen, and you are ready to believe in them. You are finding the patterns that were already there, and you now are ready to use these patterns to make magic a real part of your life. The signs and the wonders are all around you. You have fine-tuned your senses to recognise them for what they are – see the supernatural in what is natural and *already here around you*.

Remember that the world about you is not a mechanical device, it is no brass polished orrery on the desk of an omnipotent creator. Nor are we. Unpredictability is hard-wired into change, so allow the unpredictable to happen. You cannot control how something happens, but you can create the moment that starts the magic. It is perhaps not the wing of a butterfly but that of a moth – Mother Shipton's moth – that flaps a wing and starts the magic that crosses continents. Humans are so wonderfully unpredictable and strange, and you cannot predict the outcome of an event with any real sense of accuracy. You can only surmise how it might be – put the wish out there – but there is a deep and unexpected link between nature's ability to self organise and the butterfly effect, the effect of small changes. There *is* pattern and structure within order and chaos, and each action we take feeds itself back into effect without us even realising it. By making magic happen, by sensing it and sharing it with others, it feeds back into your awareness of the Source and your ability to do ever more magical things. Like Mandelbrot's fractals* there is replication of the patterns at ever smaller and smaller scales, so you start to identify the patterns. You start to recognise the embedded magic within what you do, and the larger scale as it spreads out around you. Seemingly random, the replication is identical and infinite. Pattern formation is woven into the very fabric of the universe. Its name is magic, and it all comes from, and returns to, the Source.

You are now the guide as well as the traveller, and you can use this knowledge for betterment, for success, for life. You are now the Source of your own magic. Remember, share the knowledge and live magically.

Thank you. See you around the Source.

Ursula James

---

* A mathematical set which forms a geometric pattern within which shapes are a seeming infinite number of smaller repeating shapes all the same.

EPILOGUE

*T*he final chapter was written in the shadow of a death. She, too, was called Ursula. My aunt. My namesake. Her life had been long and in it she had done what she pleased. Her laugh was that of a child and she remained interested in everything and everyone until the end. It was not until she knew that she was dying that she found out how many friends she had – how many people cared, and had loved and would miss her.

I sat with her in the final days, and watched her spirit leave two days before the strong heart in her tiny body stopped beating. 'Take the pictures from the walls, and pack my bags. I have to go now. You can't come with me this time,' she said to me. I sat with her in her moonlit room into the night, and watched her as she plucked stars from the air around her and pulled them towards her body. She smiled. I held her hand until she slept and I wished her a safe journey.

Ursula had always said that she wanted to die alone, and she got her wish. Surrounded by care and love, she still set off on her final journey alone. She was a woman who had always got her own way – and this final act was no different. I got the call when I was on the train back to my own home. She had gone. The carers telephoned me to say that they had made her ready, and placing flowers all around her, had opened the windows to let her go.

I shall miss her.

Ursula Marzinski
Born 16 November 1924
Died 29 May 2010

Mother Shipton's story

IN HER OWN RITE

Handwritten in trance by Ursula James without her intervention or intercession. 'My hand wrote the words, but they came directly from Mother. She guided the pen, while I got the cramp.'

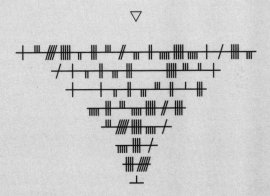

*I*t is quite easy to be distracted when you are looking down on the top of your own head – especially when it is on fire. That's when the papist bastard Wolsey's raven swallowed me whole. There I was, all peaceable like, watching my body as it caught flame. I watched the halo as my hair caught fire and smiled to myself, seeing an echo on what had, until recently, been my face. I leaned out over the head of the gargoyle cornering the tower of St Michael-Le-Belfry to get a better look. That's when it caught sight of me. I neither heard nor saw it coming. I was carried far from York, far away in the belly of that stinking raven before it shat me out into the centre of a dark, fetid cave. I can't even *begin* to tell you how annoyed I was. It had taken much planning to separate my spirit away from my body well enough for me to still be able to walk to the pyre and move it convincingly in the fire whilst my body burned. I suppose it was my own fault, I should have got away there and then but I admit to a certain curiosity. So would you in the same situation. My own vanity had got me onto the bonfire. If I had only stuck to local divination and not mentioned that his grace the Cardinal Wolsey would never set foot in York then I would probably have survived to an even ruder old age. Mind you, it hadn't hurt, becoming spirit – but to be shat out in a lime cave, that I hadn't foreseen. Some prophetess I turned out to be! This was going to be a problem. The lime in the shit fixed me to the floor of the cave, and the cave dripped more lime. An eternity in the crap. Not what I would have chosen for myself. I had to do something quickly before my spirit decayed. Like all others it needed the desires of others to sustain it. Mine more than most as my life had been that of healer.

So, I took stock of my surroundings. I knew them well. I had returned to Knaresborough, the locality of my birth. I could see a cave and its valley about it, and even though the cave was sealed from humankind and stinking like the devil's own midden, it was bordered by a beautiful place. The river and a natural park encircled the cave. It would be safe enough for what I needed – time. This was a peaceful place. The River Nidd flowed lazily close by making an almost island of the rock in which the cave lived. So I decided. I would use the lime and grow in my own image. Here, in the middle of this cave I would grow the image of my body out of the lime – and in doing so call out to the needs of those around me. This would take some time. I knew how to wait. Ugliness had taught me patience.

There were those who, when they wrote my story, believed I had been born in the cave. They were partly right. Ursula Sontheil died and the legend that was Mother Shipton was born in that space. I took my time and shaped a body in the cave, seated on a lime throne, and surrounded it with the limey water. I now had a shape with which to call the needy into the cave – a focus for their desires.

With the body now formed, my spirit cried out for freedom. I ached to fly the length and breadth of England and into the foreign and magical land of the Celts, listening and learning on my journeys. My flights were of the mind in that dark cave, and the confinement almost maddened me. But I knew. Wait. Long released from my earthly body and freed from the needs of time, the men of religion could not touch me any more, so when my spirit was fully healed I would summon the elementals to crack open the cave. That was a good day, I can tell you. The stink of the cave gave way to good, fresh Yorkshire air, and I grew flowers around the mouth of the cave to make it more inviting. In spring I took my voice for the first journey out into the air. It was dusk. A beautiful waxing moon lit the river and the secluded pathway to the outside world. It was so good – time stood still in that moment – and I waited by the mouth of the cave next to the flowers, for I knew it wouldn't be long before she came.

And she did, a young virgin came to me. Her longing heart had opened her mind to hear me. The flowers led her to the mouth of the cave, and I followed her in. 'I see into your heart, child. Leave me a gift and you will have your desire.' Now, let's be honest, I must have been a little out of practice. On reflection I had been in the cave for around 200 years and her reaction was a natural one to hearing the sound of a voice, even if the voice came from inside her own head, and seeing the shadow of a woman encased in lime in the cave before her. Not surprisingly, she shat herself and ran away in terror. It took me a few months before I ventured out again, and this time it was no virgin, but a mother who found her way to my cave. Of course it would have to be a mother. She who had known the pain of childbirth. She who had known loss. So it was that I gave to her the child she craved. Two pure souls pulled dead from her body now shivering in unconsecrated ground had left her with no love for the Church and she was prepared to call on me for healing. A bonny lad she birthed too, and she came back to me, good as her word, with a baby rattle to hang from the cave.

So I took the wooden rattle, now attached to the womb of my cave, and turned it into stone – drip by drip. And when the rattle was completely encased, a tiny echo of life was lit within me. Her need fulfilled had turned into a spark of life, and through the lime I absorbed it. My plan was working. From then on I called to the mothers – only the mothers – all who would listen. All those whose wombs knew what it was to bear fruit, and all those whose wombs ached with emptiness. Mothers who feared death, others who wished it on their husbands. Mothers whose hands ached from the daily toil of service. Mothers whose husbands strayed. The trickle became a stream, and then the stream made its own path and so my fame grew. The long walk to the cave became part of the pilgrimage. How Wolsey would have hated it! My cave became a shrine for those for whom the Church had no place. They only offered penance and misery. I offered freedom and fulfilment. No blue dress clad my image of stone. No candles lit and services held. I did my business in the darkness and shadow of the cave.

It grew quite full round the Dropping Well, and the clothing of those who came to me changed. This was no longer the exclusive home of the poor and needy. Soon women in finery and even sometimes men too sought out the cave now. Oh, but the needs did not change, though the fashions did, and all the while I waited, collecting the fire of need from each gift given to me in thanks for a child born, a husband found, a love uncovered. Do not think for one minute that in my need I could abuse theirs. No. There are rules. Break them and you slip back into the shit. If you ask me to cause pain to another I cannot and will not do it. I can, however, turn the harm they have caused you back on to themselves. This is a lesson to be learned. And if you have patience and are willing to open your mind, I will teach you. If not, enjoy your time in the shit, because that is where you will stay. Forgive me. Too long in the lime has given me a midden-mind. It will be different when I am freed from the cave.

As I have said to you, it grew full round the cave, and the new god of commerce moved into my rock. The landowner Slingsby leased my cave to a keeper as a curiosity, who in turn began to charge money to those who wanted to visit me. At first I was angry, but then accepted it. He was a man. He could neither see nor hear me. To him, the cave was just a way of trading on the gullibility of women. How ironic – as he made money, I healed those who came to my cave. His greed protected the cave from harm, and I grew stronger. So many tokens left for the lime to absorb. With each token of light given freely to the cave I grew in life. So much need invested in each. I waited until I had enough light to rekindle a phoenix fire. Waited until the world was ready for my knowledge, and then I set out to find a woman to carry my spirit alongside her child and to birth my soul out of the darkness of the cave.

Fact is, she came to me. 'Twas only proper. Foreign in tongue, strong in mind, her body had been empty of fruit for seventeen years. She had borne a son and ached for a daughter. Her mind was free of any superstitious concerns that plagued the English. She told me outright, 'Give me a daughter, and I will give you life.' I was ready to leave the cave. Ready to be young again, to become the shadow daughter that she would never see, and for a little while to hear another called 'Mother' until I grew in years with the girl-child she was to bear. This time I would have beauty as well as knowledge – through her. It was going to be an interesting life. The daughter would share life with me, and I would share knowledge – and power – if she was strong enough to receive it.

But perhaps it would be better if I tell you my story from the beginning instead of the end – or to be more accurate the middle. I have had plenty of time in the cave to reflect, and remember. All those years alone. It will make a pleasant change being able to tell my story instead of listening to everyone else's. That much you owe me, I think, for the knowledge I impart to you is without price. So, settle down, my daughters, and those sons with enough of the mother in them to see and hear me. Listen well, for within my story is a lesson for us all. If you choose to hearken to it, you can do magic. Real magic. Not the flummery and hocus-pocus of men, but real earth magic. Even now. Even in your world of noise and bright lights, technology and travel. Oh yes, I know of your world. Do you really think things have changed for the better? Listen to my voice and decide for yourself.

My story began before I was born. Birthed to an unwed mother, I was scorned by all. My mother, Agatha, was a poor and orphaned virgin when she was taken in by the soft and pliable tongue of the priest. Oh yes, dear reader. My father was no devil with horns and a tail, as local legend would have it, but devilish none the less. He watched Agatha grow like the fruit in the bushes, wild and juicy, and when he deemed she was ripe, he plucked her. She was fifteen summers young, and ready to wed. He did not give her that chance. Seducing her with his sweet Latin tongue, his incantations entranced her and she opened her legs willingly to the priest. She did not fear for her soul, nor did she worry that his seed would take root in her womb. He told his congregation from the height of the pulpit on Sunday morn readily enough that in order for a child to be conceived, the man and woman had to be married in the sight of God. So she would be all right, then. She trusted the priest, and when she became big with child he stood in the shadow and allowed the mob of women to force her to the magistrate. They would have her punished as a prostitute, but my mother would have none of it. Agatha stood before her accusers, rude and healthy with child, and quoted scripture to the magistrate: 'Let he who is without sin cast the first stone.' In the silence that followed, she pointed out Huswife Martin from the crowd who had driven her here. All eyes followed the finger as she turned scarlet and tried to push herself back into the crowd. Agatha then walked towards the magistrate, tall in his seat, and looked him square in the eye. 'Your child lives in that belly.' The woman screamed and ran from the hall. The magistrate berated the angry women: 'There is no civil case to answer here. Leave my presence.' The priest stood half in shadow, cloaked in piety by his cowardice, and he stayed silent throughout this charade.

Agatha herself had no special powers, although others called her witch from this time. Truly, other than the fact that she listened more than she spoke, and people did not see her because of her poverty. Her knowledge about Huswife Martin had come from the other women. She had heard the rumour, and put it to use. It saved her that day, and from then on she removed herself from the village and the vicious tongues of women.

From then on, Agatha was pretty much left alone by the villagers as they feared her lack of fear. She slept in a barn by the side of the farm three miles into the countryside. Three miles was far enough for her to spend her confinement in peace. The farmer and his wife knew she was there, and were happy for her to be there – she birthed their sheep in gratitude for the shelter and they slept more peacefully with this knowledge. But then the darker rumours started. All the more so when Tom Martin's wife gave birth to a weakling boy. She told anyone who would listen that Agatha had cursed her womb that day. People believed it because they wanted to, and because there was nothing much happening that summer in the village. Stories grew of how people had seen her out in the fields, courting the devil. They had seen his tail. She had sold her soul, and she would be punished. They had seen the child which she had birthed. A child born spitting and ready to bite. A demon-child. As it was, Tom Martin came to the barn, offered her money to remove the curse. Tom loved his wife, and didn't care if the child was his or no. Agatha took pity on this gentle man. She tried to tell him that she couldn't undo something she hadn't done in the first place, but he would not listen – he could not hear. So she did the only thing she could do to remove the stone from the heart of the poor cuckold – she mumbled under her breath, and told him the curse was gone. Tom cried then, and tried to push the money into Agatha's hand, but she wouldn't take it. The child recovered. It wasn't her doing. Either way her reputation was being made. If the child died, she was a powerful witch who had laid a curse; if the child thrived, she was a powerful witch who had removed a curse. Agatha was young, but no fool, and in understanding the thinking of men she realised that her survival and mine lay in other people's beliefs. She taught me well.

When I was born, mother chose to birth me alone in the barn. It was a choice that sent out a strong message to the village women. No one had seen me born, and so they made up stories of how the devil himself had brought me from hell and laid me in my mother's arms. They told of my ugliness too. That I was foul of face, hook-nosed and born with a full set of teeth – verily the sign of a devil-child. The truth of the matter was that I was no beauty. I was quite an ordinary child, but the others viewed me as dangerous and damaged and made me ugly in their fear. In the end there was no need for mother to tell tales to protect me, the village women made them up for her. So, before I could walk, I had a reputation. Spawn of the devil, I was seen as a witch, heard as a witch, child of a fallen woman – and therefore untouchable. I could fly up the chimney and in my spite would turn women upside down – so they would say. Having said that, this suited both me and Agatha fine, and by the time I learned to walk, the farmer and his wife moved us into one of the cottages, where I grew in strength and knowledge. I learned to read by watching my father at his books, but knew I had to stay silent about it. Others would see it as yet another sign of my unnatural powers, but the truth is, my father taught me, albeit without his knowledge. I was a good student – hungry to learn. Mother bore him no malice, and he would often come and visit and play with me. He played with Mother too until he was moved from the parish. Mother never knew where he had gone, and she wasn't about to set foot in the church to ask – even if she had they would not have told her. Life was like that then.

The first twelve years of my life were easy years. I learned to read at my father's knee. I allowed the shapes on the pages to speak to me in Latin and English, and the magical form of Hebraic words and symbols from the smallest book of all which he carried constantly. He left me with a head full of fire and brimstone, Ezekiel's chariot flamed in my dreams and I avoided bushes for fear of voices. He stopped reading to me when I was nine years old, so my book learning stopped then. He would not have approved of my knowledge. I was a woman – what need did I have for book learning? It was unnatural, unholy. My hunger for the magic of words did not stop, and books remained the essence of all that is magical to me. At home I learned how to cook and sew, and how to birth the sheep. I learned what herbs to stew for food, and which to pulp for medicine. I learned to recognise the shapes in the sky and to know their names. Agatha couldn't read words, but she taught me how to read so many things. Practical skills. Real knowledge. I was an able student then, hungry for learning. Most of all Mother taught me how to disappear – completely. How to be in a crowd of people so that no one saw you. She taught me how to be silent. That was the hardest lesson of all. I had a voice and wanted to use it. I wished to ask questions and to be in the crowd. Mother taught me that this was not to be. I was a fatherless child – spawn of the devil. Untouchable. I soon withdrew from the company of other children when I saw the hate in their eyes. Why did they hate me so – they didn't even know me? Mother taught me well, and I listened.

Others fear the power in you, she would say. They know that they are shackled – shackled to their families and the Church, to the fields they plough and the men they toil for. You and I, dear child, are free. In our poverty and rejected state we have no one to tie us to their rules, and for that they are afraid. The men above all fear us. They fear that one day their women will watch us and run away into the fields and give themselves over to pleasure. They fear our strength so will try to deny us – destroy us. Mother knew best. I stayed silent, and listened to her words, night after night she would sit in silhouette by the fire. A shape-shifter teaching me how to be a watcher in the woods, a listener in the fields, a shadow in the towns and villages. Mother had learned from her seat on the edge of reason and I drew that knowledge out of her before her mind left her. I did not have beauty of form to bewitch, but through Mother I learned how to weave spells. Weave them with words and cloak myself in them. By the time I was twelve I could look into the heart of man and woman and know their needs. It would be their need that would keep me alive. Their needs would clothe me, feed me, provide me with shelter.

One year passed after my father left us, and Mother went mad with loneliness and started to talk to the stones in the field. Men came to visit her, offering money for her body, but she didn't have the heart to sell it. She lost her mind in the fields, and then one day she was taken from me. I was thirteen by then, and able to look after myself. The farmer and his wife would have taken me in for their own, but the village women threatened to turn against them. I left the farm, left the village, but I took my reputation with me. On the next market day when Farmer Adam drove his sheep for sale, I went with him. I had never travelled by cart before, and the speed it went made me dizzy. They were good people, and before I left I made for them a corn doll and placed it in the barn where I was born. I told them it would protect their sheep, and it did. Once word got round the village about what I had done, no one would have dared steal any of those sheep. I protected them, all right. I was sad to leave the farm, though. Animals read you well. They do not judge you. Still, I had no choice: with Mother gone I couldn't stay safe here alone. Huswife Martin made sure of that. They had already decided how powerful a witch I was, being Agatha's child, so my reputation trod the same path as the sheep that day. When I stepped off the cart, the farmer pressed some coins into my hand. 'From Tom Martin,' he said, and with that he left me standing in York marketplace. I watched until the cart was swallowed up in the crowd and I was completely alone.

I didn't mind my solitary state at all. Ursula Sontheil, unattached and free maiden, enjoyed her liberty and her maidenhood in those four days of the market. I knew that it couldn't last for long, and that my maidenhead was currency and I needed to buy a home. I would have to find a husband soon to give me a name and a bed. There would be no peace for me in York or anywhere until I wore the kerchief of a wife. Until then, for the four days of the market, I was free to roam York. A place full of many strange sounds and sights, full of gullible strangers ready to have their pockets lightened by stealth or entertainment. And in the middle of it all was the most marvellous sight. The Minster itself rose like a yellow mountain before me, and I stood in its shadow and stared up with my mouth wide. I walked round it, watching the men swarming over it like ants on a hill. Fragile creatures on wooden scaffolds, block and tackle hoisting stone to its resting place high in the sky above York. I cast my eyes over the men until I saw what I was looking for, and I soon found it. Strong arms and a broad back, roasted red by the strong summer sun. He had a fine rear too. All this I saw while his face remained hidden from me. I stood still and waited, calling him with my stillness to turn round and look down on me. And he did. And when he did he saw the best of me. A fine view of my bosom caused him to loosen his grip on the board he carried, and it sailed down through the air straight to me. I did not move nor did I flinch. I held his gaze throughout. The wood bounced inches before me, causing a billow of dust to rise. Still I did not move, and by the time the yellow dust had settled, he stood before me – and in his relief to see me unharmed, pulled me into his body. He would have me. He did not see ugliness, he saw a young woman with round breasts and a steady gaze. He saw a merry time in his bed, and someone to cook and sew for him. All these things I did – and willingly. I jumped over the broom and took his name, for although he worked on the Minster he was no lover of the Church and its ways.

And so I transformed myself into Mother Shipton. Wife to the carpenter. Respectable. He didn't stay with me long, but I did not rant or rail. Truth was I had no need or want for a man – and none for children. I was to be a mother in title alone. It would serve me well. I had too much to do for any of that nonsense. Besides, I would be 'Mother' to all and sundry from now on. So, I took all that Agatha had taught me, and I studied the skies. I had learned the first secret, and that was to use the sky to give hope to those who sought me out. I made balms and tinctures, and I started to prophesy to all who would pay to listen. Invisible to others, I walked the streets of York every day and I listened to her stories. I did well. By not asking for a penny I was always given much more by way of thanks – a side of beef, a bolt of cloth, I traded in good fortunes, and grew smooth and fat on it. I read not the stars, but the people who brought their need to me. I saw their story in the sky and held a mirror to the events on earth. I weaved my magic through the eyes of the goodfolk around me.

It is true that it was a magical time to be in York when I was with my Toby. The city was full of foreign merchants and exotic smells. The work on the Minster was drawing to an end, and folk were being drawn to York and the connections were all pulling together. I grew busy with maidens wanting to know the initials of their future husbands, and huswives wanting potions to stop their husbands from straying with the maidens. The Minster grew solid before our eyes, more than a structure of stone. Its form was being held together by old magic. Leylines were pulled from their routes through the earth, drawn up the walls and bent into the struts supporting the vaulted ceilings. The very air within groaned with magic – old magic. This was magic drawn from a book which was older than Christianity itself, and added to by popes. I knew this. I had glimpsed this book and recognised its power. I read how this church and many others had natural magic trapped within its walls and numbers.

So, how did a humble huswife come by this knowledge? I rescued it from the Church. It called on me to set it free. When the interior of

the church was being finished, local women were employed to sweep
out the endless yellow dust. I walked among them, nodding greetings
to those I knew, and watching those I did not. My reputation was
already well made by then, and no one troubled me as I wandered
around. It was then I saw the book. Perhaps heard rather than saw.
It called to me – sang a siren song pulling me forward. I recognised
it straightaway. Piled up with others, and ready to be carried out by
the lackeys of the priests, I knew I was looking at a grimoire. I knew,
because my father had shown one to me. Much smaller that one was,
but I knew how to recognise and read it because of him. Maybe the
legend is true, maybe my father was no man but a demon in man's garb.
This Avalonian Grimoire called out to me for rescue, its power crushed
by the holy books surrounding it. I followed its song on its passage
deep into the Minster. Eventually I was observed by a fat priest, whose
tongue pushed me away. I turned to the women who were around me,
and smiled grimly. They turned away and as one began to brush, brush
towards the Minster door. The cloud they created gave me my idea.
I left quietly to return early the next morn. The Minster was not yet
locked, and I knew that I would have one chance. I entered before
Matins and lit a fire at the south end. Just a small one, where little
damage could be done, but it was enough to attract the attention of
all the faithful who came to early prayers. I snatched the book from its
prison, and carried it under my cloak and all the way home. The smoke
and the dust hid me from view, and I joined the crowds outside who
had been drawn by the smoke of the fire. I dispersed when the others
did. My face was a mask of calm. No one followed.

On entering my room, I locked the door, and laid out my prize
on the bed, still wrapped in my cloak. I laid it down in the same way
you would a child, and with the same feeling of love and awe I had
seen in mothers newly delivered. I can even now recall the feeling
of holding the simple sheepskin cover, and then tracing the symbols
and shapes hidden beneath its thickness. I felt forbidden shapes
appearing beneath my fingertips, forms which caused my heart to race
in fear. I opened the book. The thick parchment pages were blank. I
hid the book beneath the floorboards in the room I had shared with

Toby and returned to the sunlight, rejoining the last of the crowd outside.

I had recently befriended a street Moor, a reader of the sky and a spy for the Spanish court (so he told me). His itinerant wanderings followed pilgrims and he was skilled and ready to give the crowds what they craved. In his cups, I learned from him how he would write messages for his masters and the contents would disappear before his eyes. He carried these blank sheets through Europe, and the words could be made to reappear with vinegar and gall. It took me a while to get the mixture right, and I wasn't about to ask the Moor for his receipt. I valued my life and the secrets of the book were calling to me from under their sheep's clothing. I boiled the gall from the strongest, tallest oaks, and used the finest wine vinegar. Dabbing the pages gently, I brought the words back to life.

I took no further heed of the Minster, and it took none in me. No alarm went up for the missing book, and I claimed her as mine. I would care for her and understand her and nurture her. She was as a child to me. Toby had long since warmed his buttocks on the belly of another woman who would soon bear him a son. I bore him no malice, and when the time came, I helped son Sam into the world. I needed all the friends I could get, and had no fear of being alone now I was known as Mother. No man troubled me, and I paid my rent and kept myself peaceable with my neighbours. They came to me when they needed something, and I gave them what they wanted. With the book I grew in cunning and lore. I absorbed its contents, and my knowledge grew.

The book taught me how to read the skies, how to preserve life and how to take it. Some of its knowledge was written forth and back, but the symbols were already familiar to me. Many pages had notes made by different hands. It took me time, but I learned to read this book as it should be read. It had travelled across lands and ages, from Egypt to Samaria and through Europe and home to Avalon, changing all the way. I learned the book was one volume of a number, each added to, and when the writer died, he would pass this book on to a successor trained in how to read it. Occasionally the book would be completely rewritten and the last one destroyed. It was a living text. I learned how the Church had absorbed some of the magic along the way and, fearing its power, twisted it to dark intent. I learned how others had brought about the end of their civilisations with its contents. Always men. Men had possessed this book before me, but most came to understand that it was the book which possessed them. I was no man. I sought not power for myself. The magic from within the book opened itself to me without my fully understanding how. The book wanted to be read by me. It became my lover, my companion, my meat and drink. I grew in knowledge, and saw this in the fear passing over the eyes of others I met on the street. I could not read it all, and did not try. The book gave me all I could take, and I protected it with gratitude, and kept the promise to pass it on to another who would understand its power.

And so I distanced myself from the others around me. I made friends with no one, but was friendly to all. I kept the secrets they shared with me but gave none in return. I required their respect, not their love. It was a lonely time, but I had little choice. Born of Agatha and ignorance I preserved my image long before the cave took me. I read the book first through my knowledge of the skies. My first lesson came in accepting who I was. The cardinal earth sign of Capricorn taught me to ground myself before attempting any of the magic I was uncovering. I learned that all cardinal signs initiate change, but the protection of Capricorn demands that the traveller seeks security and freedom from harm before making a journey. I had to accept myself and my faults to make my journey straight and true.

Next I learned about the need for a sense of home. Virgo rules the home, and her element is the earth. I reclaimed my hearth and declared myself Mother Shipton. I understood the need for others to see me as the guardian of the home, and therefore no threat to them or their kin. People needed to know where to find me and what to expect when they did.

The lesson of Aquarius came next, so I would understand the power of flux in fixing. How important it was to define the edges around your world. I learned about when to bend, when to move, when to dig in. There is strength in mutability.

Taurus came next to awaken my sensuality and to remind me

that even more important than being Mother, I was a woman. Taurus helped me reclaim myself, look back and understand how far I had already travelled, and be sure about what I was willing to give up to move forward freely. I learned not to fear the past, but to embrace it as part of my journey. I birthed Mother Shipton and allowed Ursula to die.

Sagittarius guided me from here. Mutable and energetic, its fire burned a hole in my reality. I learned how to love myself, to love others around me, and to understand those who feared this love. I stepped beyond my five senses.

Pisces then drew me closer, and taught me how to dream, and to know of the world beyond my physical limits. I learned how to fly through the air as a fish moves through water. I learned the power of dreams and how to move from the tangible into the mystical. I learned about the space between realities and how to pass through them.

I understood the power of Leo and its healing. I learned that healing is a power source, to the giver as well as the recipient. Healing takes the initiative and creates authority. I became a healer, and healed myself along the way. Those who wished me harm only hurt themselves. I sent out love and it crippled them with shame.

My last lesson came from Cancer, the protector, which taught me to create a shell surrounding and to recognise the strength it brought to me.

There were many more lessons from the sky, but not all for me. There were many more ways of reading the Avalonian Grimoire, and I studied it throughout my life. And just as the book taught me to use my five senses to create a sixth, I learned that there were five ways to read the book. I added to her pages and to the wisdom of those who followed. I waited for the next owner to come. It saddened me that it was to be a man, but I was long enough in the tooth by then to realise the time of women had not yet come. I learned that magic was a gift available to all, and could be controlled by no one person. It *has* to be shared.

I took what I needed from the sky, and drew down the Moon to create *my* heaven on earth. I made myself real through the book. Words taught me how to live on, to become in death much more than I could ever have been in life. I live in imaginings and dreams, and through the deeds inspired in others.

The anima of magic is embedded within the levels of the words. The part to be woken and given space and time, mass and energy to make your life a truly, madly, deeply magical one finds its own level now. There are more levels within, and more routes to the Source than your senses recognise. Know this: you brought your own magic to the words contained within these pages. You awaken your own powers within the limits of your understanding of the world. True magic gives you only enough understanding so you can use your knowledge safely. You will always be safe in the arms of the anima. You will learn to trust and understand this side of you, for within the five levels there is perfection. Five is the number of the perfect man, the symbol of the universe and the divine will.

When a long-revoked law was used to put me to the stake, and I used my magic to release my spirit, 'twasn't hard. The book was clear on matters of this kind. But I should have known that Wolsey knew his own magic. How else could the son of a rascal butcher have risen so high? No matter. I survived the destruction of my body.

When the fire went cold, Toby and his son tried to claim my body. The executioner would have none of it, whether through fear or greed, I couldn't tell. Bones of a witch were worth something in those days, boiled to cure ague, or simply dug into the doorframe of a house to keep evil from the door. He did as instructed by his masters, and buried them alone and at night on Turnpike Road to stop my spirit wandering and others from stealing my remains. Toby followed him, and before dawn arrived on the next day, I made my final journey by cart heading for Somerset. Toby watched as his son buried me once more and covered my remains with a Roman stone dedicated to a child. No one would trouble my bones there. I did like Toby, truly I did. He gave me all I needed and troubled me for very little. He had his son who would do right by him. Toby had done his duty to my bones and I thanked him in my heart for that. They would not be mutilated for talismans or held up for ridicule. No unresting shades wandering for me. My spirit could and did heal in the cave, and I would learn my lesson. And the book? I left it to Sam with instructions to give it to the new Queen's young alchemist when the time came. He waited twenty years, then made the longest journey of his life to Mortlake, leaving the book on the doorstep for John Dee to find when he woke. John understood the power of the grimoire, and the story of the book is still being told by Freemasons, Rosicrucians and seekers of light. It is not a book of shadow, but a book of *light* and shadow, and can only be fully understood by one who seeks power not for their own sake, but for the good of others. The grimoire has burned the hand of many men. Perhaps, just perhaps, yours is the time when its true power is revealed. Yours is a time of the ending of the Mayan calendar, a time of earth shifts and volcanoes, a time of floods and drought. Are you listening to the earth as she screams? We are all her creatures, and it is only by nurturing her will you survive. Listen to the words culled from the book and heal yourself and the earth. The book is more than words, it is thoughts and deeds, and you are already steeped in its knowledge. It is all around you in buildings and technology, in the internet and the fibre-optic leylines that carry the message. You are part of the book and the book is part of you.

No more. My time to pass on nears and I grow weary. I have so much I want you to learn, to know, whether you want to hear it or not. I know now that I erred with my prophecies – the few which actually came from my mouth. I tried to warn others of the dangers in losing sight of what it is to be human. I voiced my words in the hope that the men of the sun would hearken and change. It was not to be. Part of me always knew it, but I felt I had no choice. Many stole my name and my voice over the many years since then, put my face on bars of soap to sell them to hard-working women, and made me into a puppet for the entertainment of children. It matters not one fig. I have a second chance at life, and a voice once more, but this time I have used it to call on the women of the Moon, and those men close enough to understand her power and connection. I call on you now to connect with the power of Sister Moon, and the strength of Mother Earth, and to grow together. We are strong in our connections, and weak in our division from one another. Do not allow the men of the Sun and their love of shining gold and power to blind you from your true worth. You are made from silver, magical in strength, not inferior but superior to gold. It runs through you, and shines when you connect with others of the Moon. Would you rather be a lunatic and at peace with yourself and the world around you, or a Sun worshipper holding out their face to the Sun to be destroyed in its relentless rays? Dance in the light of the Moon, and find love for yourself and those around you in her embrace. Open your eyes to the light in the darkness, and rejoice. My prophecies are for you – individually – personally. I, the Sourceress, call to the elements within you to come together at this time and manifest.

These words of power thou hast now read,
but what didst thou bring to the feast? For reader mine
within these words are others hidden and proud with deeper
meaning. I ask thee now to which rung of Jacob's ladder didst
thou ascend? From the bottom rung of actuality you read this
as a truth, from one step up your vision grows, the higher
thou darest to ascend, the more patterns canst thou discern.
With each rung of the ladder came wisdom and fear.
I quiz thee at the end of my story – how far wilt
thou raise thyself?

USEFUL WEBSITES

To find Ursula James online
   Website: www.ursulajames.info
   Blog: www.thebookoflightandshadow.info.com
   Tweets: www.twitter.com/ursulajames
Ethical lending
   www.zopa.com
   The world's first social finance company.
   www.kiva.com
   Loans that change lives.
Ethical clothing
   www.peopletree.co.uk
   People-centred ethical clothing partners.
Recycling
   www.recycle.co.uk
   Sell or recycle your item free.
   www.freecycle.org
   Recycle your items locally free.
Volunteering
General:
   www.hodr.org
   Hands-on disaster relief – maximum impact minimum
      bureaucracy.
   www.timebank.org.uk
   Opportunities to volunteer as an individual, group or
      company.
   www.csv.org.uk
   The UK's leading volunteering and training charity.
Elderly:
   www.ageuk.org.uk
   Volunteer to help the aged in the UK community.
In hospitals:
   www.wrvs.org.uk
   Volunteering opportunities in hospitals and more.
For those with mental health issues:
   www.sane.org.uk
   Saneline.

Children:
  www.compassionatekids.com
  Volunteering with children.
  www.actionforchildren.org.uk
  Working with children.
  www.postpal.co.uk
  Write a letter to a sick child.
Animals:
  www.animal-job.co.uk/voluntary-work-with-animals
  Volunteering for animal charities at home or abroad.
Holidays:
  www.responsibletravel.com
  Home and abroad, all kinds of projects.
  www.btcv.org.uk
  UK's leading charity creating better environments where
  people feel valued, included and involved.

Ursula James is a patron of the following charities

  National Centre for Domestic Violence
  www.ncdv.org.uk

  Anxiety UK
  www.anxietyuk.org.uk

Ursula also supports the work of

  www.womenforwomen.org
  Empowering women survivors of war.

  www.warriorprogramme.org.uk
  Empowering ex-service personnel and homeless individuals
  to rebuild confidence and dignity.

And finally . . .
  www.mothershiptonscave.com
  Mother Shipton's Cave, Knaresborough – open for visitors
  from March to October.